YOU HAVE A PURPOSE

Find, Learn, Master, and Give Your Gifts to the World

WES LEE

While every precaution has been taken in the preparation of this book, the publisher assumes no responsibility for errors or omissions, or for damages resulting from the use of the information contained herein.

YOU HAVE A PURPOSE

First edition. September 5, 2020.

Copyright © 2020 Wes Lee.

Written by Wes Lee.

Contents

Contents

INTRODUCTION 9

PART I

CHAPTER 1: FIND YOUR PURPOSE

GRANDMA MOSES 13
GRANDMA MOSES'S GUIDANCE 15
GREENFIELD VILLAGE 16
STEVE HARVEY 20
PEER PRESSURE 24
RESOURCES 25
FAKE PURPOSE 27
LIVING IN THE PAST 27
GETTING SIDETRACKED 28
ABRAHAM LINCOLN'S GUIDANCE 33
REFLECTION 33

CHAPTER 2: LEARN YOUR PURPOSE

The Learning Phase 36

Michael Jordan 37

Michael Jordan's Guidance 39

The Goal of Learning Your Purpose 42

How To Learn Your Purpose Effectively 44

Phase One: Watching 46

Phase Two: Practicing 50

Phase Three: Testing 55

Why Education Is More Important Than Money 64

Always Reach Up 69

Take A Lesson From Children 75

Have Faith..78

Choosing The Narrow Gate 82

Failure Is A Blessing 83

Walt Disney's Guidance 86

Understand Your Surroundings..................................88

Try And Try Again 91

PART II

CHAPTER 3: YOUR MENTOR

TONY ROBBINS MENTOR..99

JIM ROHN'S GUIDANCE 100

TONY ROBBIN'S GUIDANCE 104

HOW TO MAKE THE MOST OF MENTORING....................105

JOHANN SEBASTIAN BACH'S GUIDANCE 110

CHAPTER 4: BUILD YOUR IDENTITY

NELSON MANDELA..116

NELSON MANDELA'S GUIDANCE 119

UNDERSTANDING INDIVIDUAL BEHAVIORS 122

GENERAL HUMAN BEHAVIORS 126

NIKOLA TESLA 135

CHOOSE YOUR PERSONALITY (ANDY WARHOL) 139

PEOPLE DO THE CRAZIEST THINGS (RANDY MOSS).............141

ANDY WARHOL'S GUIDANCE 145

CHAPTER 5: EXPAND YOUR KNOWLEDGE & CREATIVITY

MOVING CLOSER TO REALITY (RAY DALIO) 147

THE IDEA MERITOCRACY (RAY DALIO)	156
RAY DALIO'S GUIDANCE	158
RELEASE (STEVE JOBS)	158
STEVE JOBS GUIDANCE	161
HARNESS YOUR CONSCIOUSNESS (THE WRIGHT BROTHERS)	162
WILBUR WRIGHT'S GUIDANCE	166
IDENTIFY AND BREAK YOUR HABITS (STEVE JOBS)	167
IDENTIFYING PROBLEMS BUT NOT CAUSES	169
CONSIDERING THE VISIBLE AND NOT THE INVISIBLE (TESLA MOTORS)	171
ELON MUSK'S GUIDANCE	173
CONFIRMATION BIAS	175
LEARNING FROM OUR ANCESTORS	176
ALESSANDRO VOLTA'S GUIDANCE	180
THE IMPORTANCE OF PRESSURE AND REFLECTION	181
THE SIX DANGEROUS FEELINGS	185
CREATE YOURSELF	194
WARREN BUFFETT'S GUIDANCE	196
EXPAND YOUR UNIQUENESS (ED SHEERAN)	197
ED SHEERAN'S GUIDANCE	200
OUR HANDS UNLOCK OUR IMAGINATION (STEVE WOZNIAK)	201

Steve Wozniak's Guidance 205

Repurpose The Existing (Sara Blakely) 205

Sara Blakely's Guidance 208

The Importance of Accidents (Sir Alexander Fleming) 209

Sir Alexander Fleming's Guidance 213

Creativity As a System (Alan Turing) 213

Alan Turing's Guidance 216

Polarity (Taylor Swift) 217

Taylor Swift's Guidance 220

CHAPTER 6: MASTER YOUR PURPOSE

Health 228

Self-Motivation 229

Vision 230

Focus 231

Self-Control 233

Failure is Success 234

People Help People They Like 236

Overdeliver...238

Rationality 239

MANAGE YOUR RESOURCES 240
CONTRIBUTION 244
JAY-Z'S GUIDANCE 245

BONUS CHAPTER: *YOU ARE FREE*

NEXT STEPS

ALSO BY WES LEE

BIBLIOGRAPHY

Introduction

"Let others lead small lives, but not you. Let others argue over small things, but not you. Let others cry over small hurts, but not you. Let others leave their future in someone else's hands, but not you." - Jim Rohn

Each of us is born with a purpose that represents our strengths and ultimate human potential. The people that find and master their highest calling live with significant fulfillment and joy. It's that thing that you've flirted with throughout your life, it brings you immeasurable happiness, and fills you with energy.

Your purpose is where your mind wanders to and what it focuses on because it wants to, not because it has to. It comes from your unconscious and calls you to do it; ideas come from it, we dream of it, and we seem to be a different person when interacting with it. Our purpose gives us creativity, it makes us feel alive, and we need it as much as we need food and water.

The problem is that most people are not living through their purpose, their deepest desires. Many ignore its calling, don't believe in themselves enough, or talk themselves out of going after what they love. Together, we will examine the root of what you desire, how to find it, learn it, master it, and share it with others.

You're going to embark on a journey with over a dozen iconic people who have lived and mastered their highest purpose. Each of these legends will guide you through the necessary phases of attaining what fulfills you at your core. You will walk with giants, and in the process, become a giant in your own right.

Think of this as having unlimited (24-hour) access to coaching from some of the most brilliant people in their fields. Use this as a reference guide, the most convenient way to get information that's true and accurate. There are plenty of "wannabe experts" on social media; anyone with a camera can become your next "guru." However, with this guide, you have proven answers from people with proven results. Success always leaves breadcrumbs, and to do anything, you simply need to model those that have already done it. It's an honor to walk with you, help you find why you're on this planet, and help you master it so you can pay it forward and serve humanity with your gifts. With deep appreciation, Wes

Part I

Chapter 1: Find Your Purpose

"It's not enough to have lived. We should be determined to live for something." —Winston S. Churchill

Grandma Moses

You're never too old or too young to find your purpose; there's no such thing as being too late. We all have a guiding voice within us that draws us towards our meaning. All progress begins within, and when you're clear on your direction, the pieces of your life will fall in line.

When we were young, we knew our purpose. The teacher asked us what we want to *be,* and we proudly said what we believe. Our younger self wasn't trying to be *realistic*, and our thoughts were infinite.

However, as we grew older and gained more exposure to people, that inner force got drowned out by a voice of limitation. Life chips away at us, causing unhappiness, and then we lose that link to what makes us unique.

Anna Mary Robertson Moses is a legend in American fine arts and folk arts. The crazy part is that she didn't start practicing art until she was in her late seventies.

"Grandma Moses," as she was known, had a passion for embroidery. Still, she stopped when her arthritis pain prevented her from holding a needle. A few years after the death of her husband in 1927, Moses started painting.

She produced her first canvas at 76 years old and continued painting two decades after that. You can still find her work sold in the United States and overseas to this day; Moses' art is on greeting cards and various merchandise. You can see her original paintings in many museums. To give you an idea of her prowess, in 2006 her picture, *Sugaring Off,* sold for $1.2 million.

Once Grandma Moses connected with her real purpose, her life transformed quickly. Check this out, at first, her art was hanging in a store when art collector Louis J. Caldor saw them and purchased each one.

Just one year later, some of Moses's paintings got displayed at the Museum of Modern Art in New York City in an "unknown artists" exhibit. Shortly after the exhibition, she held the first one-woman show in New York. Then, the following year, her art was in Gimbels, a famous New York department store.

Grandma Moses's Guidance

"I look back on my life like a good day's work, it was done, and I feel satisfied with it. I was happy and contented; I knew nothing better

and made the best out of what life offered. And life is what we make it, always has been, always will be."

—Grandma Moses

Greenfield Village

Many of the highest achievers in history have confessed to feeling a compelling internal drive. John D. Rockefeller, for example, one of the wealthiest men to ever live, expressed his belief that God gave him his money. Rockefeller believed that part of his purpose was to change the world with his wealth. This definiteness of purpose is core to his philanthropic efforts, such as the University of Chicago.

Many may see an inner force as "magic" or "imagination." Still, our internal spirits are real because we're all born entirely different than anyone who existed before us and will exist after us. You and I are creations that will never exist again. When you were young, what were you drawn towards doing?

Whatever you were drawn to as a child has shaped your mind and created unique grooves that make up who you are. Your calling wants you to express yourself strongly in specific directions; you also feel pushed away by other paths in life. When we find our calling, it's an overwhelming feeling of destiny. Working within your purpose feels effortless, it requires no thought, and it looks impossible to others.

When you came into existence, you were born with a mission; we are all born with one. Your life's work is to nurture its growth. It has an energy that pulls you, and regardless of what you do in life, it always tries to lure you towards it. The stronger the feeling, the closer you are to your life's work. The reason we feel negativity is because we're straying far from our purpose. We stray from our mission because of social pressures; we don't want to seem weird or look different. Our lives are influenced by those that we spend the most time around.

When I was little, I loved spelling. I'll never forget 4th grade when I kept winning spelling competitions. Writing can't exist without spelling, and this was my clue that I was close to my purpose. Then the most challenging field trip of my young life occurred. If you visit Michigan, there's a great spot called Greenfield Village; it feels like stepping back into the 1800s.

All week I was excited about a spelling competition we were having in the Greenfield Village one-room schoolhouse. Our class got split up into teams, and my group was thrilled that they had me. I was confident, almost arrogant, that we would win.

Fast forward to Friday morning; the competition is going down. I got up each time and nailed my words, as people dropped like flies. You would have thought we already won the contest the way I was strutting around. Then, my 5th time up to spell, I butchered the word. I don't remember what I spelled, but I remember how it felt.

I could feel the air sucked from the room as I sat down, eliminated. My team lost, and I stopped caring about reading and writing for almost 20 years. After that experience, I lost contact with my purpose and believed others who told me to get my college degree, or I would end up a loser. People pushed their expectations on me, and I dutifully obeyed.

Because of listening to others, I transitioned through five different careers, made an astounding amount of money in one, but felt empty. I had no sense of direction in my life, helping me navigate. I broke the link with my uniqueness and wandered through life aimlessly. That is until I left the last job I'll ever have, and decided that I will only live for my passion (writing) for the rest of my life.

Once you reconnect with your purpose from your childhood, our goal is to reach the level of legends. It doesn't matter when you reconnect with your purpose, as long as you reconnect. Our passion is always with us, seeking to propel us forward, it's ready for you whenever you're ready for it.

After reconnecting with your passion, the second phase is to examine the work you perform already. Many people split their life into different compartments such as, who we are at work, and who we are outside of work. Your vocation is more than just making money to live; it needs to be your source of happiness and fulfillment. Don't continue to devote your time to work in the hopes that you'll someday retire and enjoy life. Pleasure, satisfaction, and career are not mutually exclusive.

Steve Harvey

On the subject of *vocation*, it's a Latin word meaning to call. It's much more than what you *do*; it's what speaks to you. In 2019 I was at a business growth conference with Steve Harvey. Most people think of Steve as a comedian. Still, that evening he got down to business and shared some wisdom about finding your purpose.

He told me about being homeless, living out of his car, wanting to be on T.V. since he was a child. Then one day, someone close to him took him to a comedy club and encouraged him to get up on stage. That day, the Steve Harvey we know and love was born. Steve told me he knew that he found who God wanted him to be that day.

He said, "your gift comes naturally, live in your gift, and ask yourself what is my gift?" Steve also said, "God gives you a gift; make room for it." And one thing he didn't know back then was that to make money, you only need to provide a service or sell something. Finally, he said, "The more money you have, the more you can help, and the more God will help you, help people." Take his words to heart as we connect with your most profound purpose.

Lastly, understand that your path will never be direct. Your vocation is a lifestyle and a lifelong pursuit.

Begin at a high level and choose something that has a general correlation to your purpose. It's crucial to value *learning* over *money* and be willing to start over. It's more important to begin again on the right path than continuing to go the wrong way.

At the start, it's more important to learn who you are, while growing your new skills. As time passes, your vocation will become less general and more specific. You'll feel the draw towards different fields of knowledge. Interest and intrigue will overtake you as you move through your vocation with the wonder of a child.

Your prowess in your vocation will reach a level where you surpass the people around you. You'll crave new heights of knowledge, mentors, and liberties to pursue your purpose more deeply. In our world of instant gratification, those that focus on a single mission are rare. Information comes easy, "shiny objects" are everywhere to distract the masses, attention spans have dropped, and there's no shortage of ways to combat boredom.

With unprecedented access to information, there's also been an expansion of global issues that need solving; the world needs your gifts. The world pays very well for those that master a single purpose, and it's much better to excel at one thing than be good at many things; the jack of all trades gets paid like a clown. The essence of freedom is people being able to express who they are while providing their diverse gifts. The human race needs diversity; we survive and thrive because of our differences. By developing your uniqueness, you contribute to the greatness of our whole race.

Many will never find their purpose, and many will leave this world without giving the full expression of their gifts to humanity. If you choose to take off the guise that hides who you are, if you wish to listen to your calling, you'll walk the path of legends, and become a free individual.

As you find your purpose, you'll run into five challenges that you must overcome. These challenges are the reason your journey isn't a straight line from A to B. We're going to address how to overcome them, in turn. These obstacles come in no particular order, but you'll encounter each of them at some point.

Peer Pressure

The **first** obstacle is peer pressure. The book of Proverbs, in the Bible, captures how to handle peer pressure effectively. In chapter 1, verse 7, there's a portion that says, "fools despise wisdom and instruction." Peer pressure is a sin that fools commit; these fools want to take you down a dark path away from your destiny. The Bible suggests not to walk in the way of these people because they set their trap for their life.

When I was in high school, I was the guy who did what others wanted so that they would like me. It was a constant cycle of stupid stunts to get a laugh, but none of the people around me respected me. Back then, I didn't listen to my inner calling because I believed all of the external voices around me. It's no coincidence that I was at the lowest point in my life, with no car, driver's license, job, meaningful relationship, or education.

Crazier still, It was six years after high school when I received my high school diploma. Five of those years, I was playing World of Warcraft for 15 hours a day. Everyone around me told me that was the thing to do, so I did. We were all a group of fools that didn't want wisdom or instruction, and until an intervention occurred, I may have never found my voice.

Resources

The **second** obstacle is your resources. Daymond John has a great book called *The Power of Broke,* where he talks about his resources growing up. John started a clothing line called FUBU in New York. The company started in his home in the early '90s when internet marketing wasn't a thing. Daymond was broke, but it was the greatest thing that happened to him, one of his blessings. Without a lot of resources, we need to get resourceful, and that's what Daymond did.

Without the resources to get himself in storefronts or on billboards in New York, he used spray paint to tag his logo in high-traffic areas. Without the resources to get himself promoted on T.V., he negotiated with music artists, getting them to wear his clothes in their videos. Before Uber and Lyft, Daymond used some of his profits to buy a van, driving people around New York, promoting his clothing line, and selling it out of the back.

As you find your purpose, you may come face to face with the feeling that you don't have the resources. Remember that the people who break this obstacle down get resourceful.

I lived in over 20 places by the time I was 20 years old. If having money and high-level connections were the only way to start achieving success, I would have been out from the start. You don't need more resources; you need to repurpose what you already have. By not having the world handed to us, our advantage is that we learn to grow, control, and keep our success.

Take most child actors, for example, they came into a massive amount of success, became known throughout the world, and starred in iconic movies such as Home Alone. Where are many of them now? Who knows! Acting might be their purpose, but they received much of their success before they were ready to control it. How can anyone take care of a *lion* before they knew how to take care of a *house cat*? Many times, what comes fast, goes fast.

Fake Purpose

The **third** obstacle is the fake purpose. The world isn't short on false teachers, services, and products. We are so interconnected, with access to so much information that it can seem overwhelming to try to decide what path to take. Anyone with a camera can turn it on and become your next "expert." Following what fake teachers say leads us down the wrong path, costing us loads of time and money.

Warren Buffett once said, "Don't ask the barber whether you need a haircut." The same wisdom applies to fake teachers. These "barbers" are everywhere, and they drown out the only voice that matters, your inner voice. In a world of fake, you need to dig deep, turn off all of the suggestions everyone has for you, and listen to yourself; that tiny inner voice is your guide. Do you know the surefire way to spot a fake? If they don't *live* what they're telling you, they're fake.

Understand, just because something is fake doesn't always mean that there are wrong intentions. Plenty of well-meaning people unintentionally set others back with their ignorant advice. You're out to find your purpose, so you need to be able to sift through the noise and identify what's real.

Today my wife was scrolling through Instagram when a girl popped up in her feed to share that she and her husband paid off all of their debts. Other people were congratulating her, cheering for her, and asking her how she did it. The girl said that they achieved it because COVID-19 forced her and her husband to stay inside and stop going out to spend money. Also, the unemployment checks and government stimulus program gave them enough extra income to pay all of their debts. Then, in the following sentence, the girl said, "My husband and I can't decide if we want to buy a 2nd house or buy a 2nd car."

Can you see the fake advice cleverly hidden in this story? First, paying off bad debt is an excellent thing. However, the root of bad debt is bad choices.

Debt can also be positive if it puts money back in our pocket, such as borrowing money to purchase an investment. How many times would you take a loan out for $1000 if it paid you $5000?

A big red flag is that she said COVID-19 forced them to stay inside and not spend money. What that means is that they couldn't find anyone to take their money (or debt). So, these two people were more than willing to go out, spend money they didn't have, and get into more debt, but circumstances prevented it. This behavior suggests that these two people don't have the discipline to remain free of bad debt, and consume less, which means they can't teach others how to get out of debt.

Next, this couple got out of debt using temporary relief funds. It's not a sustainable plan to rely on the government to bail us out because they're in massive debt themselves. The stimulus funds and additional unemployment income paid by the Federal government was approved because the government knows that *spending* stimulates the economy (the government wants people to get in debt).

Finally, the couple can't decide if they want to buy a 2nd house or a 2nd car now that they're debt-free. For anyone who has recently broken the grip of bad debt, they know that they're basically at $0. How could someone have the income to buy a home or a car immediately? They can't, without more debt. The couple is looking for the next place they can give their money to, the next spot they can get into debt because they haven't truly learned how to operate without it.

And if they don't live it, they can't teach other people how to do it.

If this couple gave other people advice on how to get out of debt, those people might follow it and waste years of precious time that could have gone towards their real purpose. This obstacle was longer than the others, but I need to emphasize the importance of the fake teachers in this world, so you don't end up wandering in the jungle. One more time, if they don't *live* it, they can't teach you how to *do* it.

Living In The Past

The **fourth** obstacle is living in the past. "I had Amazon stock in 1997 if I hadn't sold it, I would be rich right now!" Have you heard people talk like that? And have you heard of a man named Ron Wayne? Most haven't, however, he was the (little known) 3rd owner of Apple with Steve Jobs and Steve Wozniak. In 1976, Wayne was frightened of the enormous debt that Steve Jobs was amassing to build Apple.

Besides the debt, Jobs and Wayne didn't see eye to eye on Apple, ultimately resulting in Wayne selling his 10% ownership in Apple for $800. Today, a 10% ownership in Apple would be worth about $100 billion. Still, Wayne has repeated time and again that he doesn't live with regret and wouldn't change his decision if he could.

Wayne went on to say, "If I had stayed with Apple and accepted the limitations on my philosophy of life, I could have well ended up the richest man in the cemetery. I was in my 40s; these kids were whirlwinds. It was like having a tiger by the tail."

Change is inevitable, and we must be able to release ourselves from any ties to people, jobs, and companies. The past exists as a teacher, it won't change, but we can use it to improve our present and our future. What life changes are occurring for you right now? By being present, you won't miss critical opportunities. Be fluid, like a river, ready to change, staying unattached to everything that doesn't serve you.

If you feel forced to make a decision, as Wayne did, don't live with regret once you make a choice. Wayne went on to live a beautiful life in Nevada, free from remorse for his decision with Apple. Although some people have written about him, calling him the most unlucky man on Earth, if they were in his shoes at the time, many of those people would have made the same decision.

Your life's purpose evolves as you evolve; it isn't rigid. Once we freeze ourselves in our habits, time passes, and we lose the sense of purpose that sparked so much wonder for us as children. Let the past serve its only purpose, to be your teacher.

Getting Sidetracked

The **fifth** and final obstacle is getting sidetracked. Before politics, Abraham Lincoln was a lawyer. He taught himself law by reading William Blackstone's Commentaries on the Laws of England. Lincoln was accepted to the bar in 1837 and made a move to Springfield, Illinois, where he practiced law in the John T. Stuart law firm.

In 1844, Lincoln formed a partnership with a man named William Herndon to practice law together. Admittedly, Lincoln and Herndon's styles of law varied; however, they created a close relationship (professionally as well as personally).

Lincoln was doing well as a lawyer, but it wasn't his real purpose. There also wasn't enough work in Springfield, Illinois, so Lincoln needed more income. To supplement himself, he followed the court through various seats in the county of Illinois. Nonetheless, Lincoln wasn't born to be a lawyer.

From 1847 to 1849, Abraham Lincoln served in the U.S. House of Representatives. This brief move into national politics was nothing astounding, and very short. As part of the Whig party, he was the only representative from Illinois. Lincoln showed loyalty to the Whig but had almost no allies.

In Lincoln's term, he opposed the Mexican-American War, opting to support Zachary Taylor for president. By speaking out against the war, Lincoln's home state didn't like him. He didn't run for a second term and went backward, returning to Springfield to resume his law career. As you can see here, Lincoln was flirting with his purpose but fell off his path.

In the 1850s, the railroad industry was expanding west, and Illinois became an essential stop for many companies; Lincoln lobbied for the Illinois Central Railroad as its attorney. Other clients began desiring to work with Lincoln due to his success in several cases. Among the clients were banking, insurance, and manufacturing companies. Aside from business cases, Lincoln also worked in criminal trials. With this success, Lincoln could have easily continued down his path as an attorney, but he would have missed his life's calling.

In 1854, the Kansas-Nebraska Act came into law; this act repealed the Missouri Compromise, allowing individual states and territories to choose their position on slavery. The bill also created strong opponents in Kansas and Illinois, which gave power to the Republican Party.

This act was the catalyst that pushed Lincoln back into politics, swaying his views on slavery towards anger, provoked by unfair treatment. Shortly after, Lincoln joined the Republican Party in 1856.

Back in the political arena, Lincoln challenged U.S. Senator Stephen Douglas for his seat. Lincoln criticized Douglas, the Supreme Court, and President Buchanan for supporting slavery, and he declared, "a house divided cannot stand."

Understand that although the state legislature elected Douglas, the attention Lincoln received thrust him into national politics.

Because of Lincoln's political clout, Illinois organized a campaign in support of Lincoln for the 1860 presidential election. Chicago's Republican National Convention on May 18th was a pivotal day. Lincoln made himself a name when he defeated known candidates,

New York's William Seward, and Ohio's Salmon P. Chase.

Lincoln was nominated because his views on slavery were moderate; he supported improvements to the nation's infrastructure, and he was in favor of protective tariffs.

The general election was challenging, but Lincoln defeated Stephen Douglas, John C. Breckinridge of the Northern Democrats, and the Constitution Party's John Bell. Earning nearly 40 percent of the popular vote and 180 of 303 Electoral College votes, Lincoln won the presidential election.

Can you imagine if President Lincoln never went back into politics? The world would have been worse for it. Lincoln is considered by many to be the greatest United States president ever to live. He was known for using every presidential power he possessed to enact change. Most notably, Lincoln won the civil war and changed U.S. history by freeing the slaves with the emancipation proclamation.

None of this would have happened if he ignored his real purpose and remained a successful attorney in Illinois. Your obstacle is getting on the wrong path, but similar to Lincoln, you need to treat it as a life or death commitment to leave your current way and pursue your true calling.

Abraham Lincoln's Guidance

"Those who deny freedom to others deserve it not for themselves." -Abraham Lincoln

Reflection

Nothing good comes from moving in a direction that isn't your real purpose. Straying from it, you can become shackled by the whims and interests of others. Some companies hold a paycheck over others and believe they own them. You don't deserve to wander down the wrong path and let others dictate your time.

Most people give up on their actual path because of money, shiny objects, and instant gratification. Lincoln had no guarantees of political success, but he had business clients lined up to pay for his services as an attorney. Despite Lincoln's success as a lawyer, he would have ended up at a dead end.

If you feel anxious, frustrated, irritable, or on edge, it's your inner voice telling you that you're on the wrong path. Often, you'll have to move backward temporarily, which may include pay cuts and the awkwardness of learning something new. However, with patience, you'll realize that it was worth the sacrifice because the rest of your life will be that of fulfillment.

Your journey is not just about you. You have blessings to give the world, you are a person of infinite potential, and you don't belong to yourself. You're a piece of the universe, make a dent in it with your purpose.

Chapter 2: Learn Your Purpose

"If you can tune into your purpose and really align with it, setting goals so that your vision is an expression of that purpose, then life flows much more easily."
—Jack Canfield

The Learning Phase

Once you've finished traditional education, your practical training begins. When we choose a purpose, we start down a specific road and immerse ourselves in its ways. We start learning the vocabulary, nuances, and the accepted "norms" of the field. Every time we move to a new path, we're starting over and beginning this phase again.

It's critical to find your purpose and stick with it because this *learning* phase will cost us time whenever we start over. Also, starting over creates a lack of confidence, and we're at risk of developing fears and learning blocks that can become bad habits.

Before you become a person who jumps between jobs or hops from one "opportunity" to the next, you need to learn your purpose. You need to master the skills, vocabulary, and mindset to become a person who moves freely and independently through your life's mission. As you learn your purpose, you'll face incredible creative challenges that will force you to grow. Remember, level 10 people don't sweat level 5 challenges; you're about to become level 10 with your purpose.

Michael Jordan

Jordan found his purpose early but learning it didn't prove to be easy. He made the game look effortless when we watched him in the NBA; however, it's easy to forget that he didn't get to that level by accident. Jordan had an ego, and a hunger to be a legend.

The hunger started from a young age, with a desire to beat his brother Larry on the court. And it carried through the NBA when Jordan put Magic Johnson in his place in the NBA finals. Jordan even got cut trying out for the basketball team in his sophomore year of high school. Regardless, he put the same effort into practice that he put into every game.

When Michael was at practice with the Bulls, he'd give himself a more challenging practice routine than required. Jordan practiced as he played, he would do three-point shooting drills and always ask for pressure from Scottie Pippen or Horace Grant. Michael wanted to perform under pressure because it accelerated his learning.

The team knew Jordan would never give up until he won; in everything, not just basketball. When Michael couldn't find something challenging enough, he'd simply create additional challenges for himself. Even with drills and coaching that others would resist or think they're too good for, Michael accepted it graciously.

In the 1994-1995 season, Jordan transitioned from basketball to baseball temporarily. Although baseball wasn't his purpose, Jordan practiced as hard as he did for basketball. This transition was a period where Jordan started over, and the learning of this sport cost him time practicing basketball. Nonetheless, he worked with the Chicago White Sox batting coach (Walt Hriniak), every day, until his hands bled.

Baseball wasn't even his purpose, but he valued learning so profoundly that he was willing to practice until he bled. If he was ready to suffer so much for baseball, can you imagine the effort he must have put in basketball? It's no wonder why Jordan mastered basketball at such a deep level.

Michael Jordan's Guidance

"Learning's a gift, even when pain is your teacher." – Michael Jordan

Michael Jordan was always going through stages of development. Most stories highlight his glory but don't discuss the days of intense effort to get there. Basketball fans loved watching him play for three hours, but nobody would want to watch him work on his fundamental skills in practice for the same three hours. Crowds want huge dunks, close games, and highlight-worthy moments; they don't want to see everything behind the "curtain" that leads up to that level of skill.

It's in those dull moments of practice that our minds are reshaping and planting the foundation for our achievements to come. By studying the best, we can take insights for ourselves and succeed in learning our highest purpose. There's no shortcut to bypass the learning phase of our mission, and we need to be willing to struggle and mold ourselves.

When we're young, we begin learning almost immediately after we were born. Each of us moves through the same (prolonged) state of needing people to take care of us. In our childhood, we learn to read, write, and learn a little about a lot of general subjects such as art and history. The majority of this learning goes without any practical experience, and we mostly intake information without practicing it at any level, more in-depth than the surface.

When we finish traditional education, our ingrained habit is to learn without doing. We know how to absorb information, but many of us are weak at applying it. To excel at anything, we need to practice it, not just read about it or learn it from teachers. So, the way many people learn as children makes it more difficult for them to practice their purpose as adults.

For those that adjust, they can succeed, as Michael Jordan did. For others, they make mistakes and create more issues for themselves. Getting caught in the problems of life takes our focus away from the reflection necessary to process our life experiences. Learning your purpose will always be done uniquely; there's no single recipe that everyone can follow.

To bypass the mistakes of others and deeply learn your purpose, there's wisdom you can follow that has proven right. We'll go through each piece of knowledge, but lets first get clear about your end *goal* for learning your purpose.

The Goal of Learning Your Purpose

Quicken Loans has several core philosophies, one being, "Numbers and money follow; they do not lead." The goal of learning and mastering your purpose isn't money, numbers, or credentials. The real gift is who you become.

Whenever we start something new, we're out of the loop, ignorant, and unaware of the rules. At the start of the learning phase, we only have our narrow experiences and what we've learned as a foundation of knowledge. Similar to Michael Jordan, moving from college basketball to the NBA, we have much to learn. However, over time, we learn the real truths and replace our original assumptions.

As we go from an outsider to an insider in our field, we learn to accept constructive feedback. We also practice, fail, succeed, and trade time for knowledge. As we pass through these trials, we become equipped to take on more challenging tasks, we gain discipline, and we triumph over ourselves.

To learn your purpose, you need to choose your vocation because of its educational value. What can you involve yourself in that has enormous learning potential? Don't follow the path of people who want to climb the "ladder" of their careers. The small pay increases of that path are nothing compared to the rewards from gaining practical experience.

Like Jordan, how can you make learning your purpose more difficult for yourself? How can you add additional pressure to sharpen your skills? Don't choose the path that seems effortless. Jordan could have gone to practice and met the requirements for 3-point drills, instead of making each session more difficult for himself. He would have been playing it safe, never unlocking his next-level of potential; his level 10 self. In that case, Jordan would have been just another pro basketball player instead of a legend.

Adopt this way of being into your life, see your life as a wondrous journey, and approach the world with an open mind, just as you did when you were young. Learning your purpose is an adventure with much more substance than on the job training.

How To Learn Your Purpose Effectively

By focusing on the educational value of your purpose, instead of the money, titles, or prestige, you're correctly aligning yourself to learn effectively. You're now ready for the wisdom necessary to master your most profound purpose successfully. At a broad level, whenever we start anything new, we watch, practice, and then test.

As you learn your purpose, you'll embark on a journey different than anyone else. This practical education will involve the mixture of unique decisions you've made leading up to this point; you'll apply some of your prior knowledge to your learning. You'll watch differently than others, you'll practice in your unique way, and you'll test your new ideas.

Depending on the purpose you're drawn to, you may value watching, practicing, and testing differently. For instance, a basketball player highly values practicing, while the biologist puts more emphasis on observing (watching) and testing. Let's begin your indoctrination with the first phase, watching.

Phase One: Watching

Once you've found your purpose, transitioning into it involves the same sequence of steps that you'd follow to transition into anything new. The first phase is becoming accustomed to the new environment, which will have its own culture. The culture will involve accepted "norms," systems, and social structure.

Have you noticed that each generation wants to do things differently than the previous generation? There's been a silent rebellion against our parent's generation, just as our parents went against their parent's generation—for example, the shift from the industrial era to the information age.

No matter what field you choose, unique connections and realities exist that you need to understand and observe. A great mentor once said, "you need to be *interested* instead of *interesting*." The single most significant error people make in the initial learning stage is trying to be the most impressive person in the room. Focusing on impressing others takes the minds' focus away from watching and understanding the norms, systems, and social structure that existed long before you arrived.

When you start into your purpose, keep a low-profile. By watching, your only task is to study that which already exists around you; the realities. Don't set any expectations, and don't let any praise you receive cloud your attention. You're biding your time and learning; because learning is the single most important reason you're devoting your time to that vocation.

First, watch how the people around you get things *done*. A lot of environments have "best practices," and the majority of people are resistant to change. Because of people's resistance, watch for routines in their behavior. You're looking for the *spoken* and *unspoken* ways of the environment, which often come from the most prominent people in the field (CEOs, owners, experts, and top officials).

Who in your space seems untouchable? Observe their actions, and identify what behaviors bring them so much success in that field. Who is struggling?

These people are vital to your progress because they're the people making the crucial mistakes you need to avoid.

Second, every environment has unique relationships. For the people who are doing exceptional, whose in their network? Are you expected to follow a chain of command, while others are allowed to bypass it? You must understand where the power flows in your field. Reaching the pinnacles of your purpose, and expanding your freedom depends on watching the flows of power and influence that can help you ascend.

Remember, at this phase; you're watching people. Once you reach the freedom to begin *testing* different angles of your purpose, you'll have the freedom you need to make changes to the culture. Right now, you need time to accumulate information. In this phase, serve others, regardless of how small the task is, seek to deliver value.

When you serve others, you build rapport, trust, and gain the information necessary to make accurate decisions. The people that shoot themselves in the foot are the people who *assume* they already know.

Michael Jordan followed this well when he took coaching in basketball. He could have thought he knew better, and he could have assumed his way was the best way. However, he practiced the fundamentals and accumulated information.

Jordan was once watching footage of Scottie Pippen outplaying Larry Bird (late in his career); Early in Pippen's career, Bird beat him consistently. Watching the tape, Jordan said to the coach: "You would let me know if someone was beating me like Pippen is beating Bird, right?" Jordan was practicing watching his environment, accumulating information, and staying open-minded to constructive feedback. Michael was admitting that he (a legend) can get beat, and he always wanted to know the reality of his surroundings.

Phase Two: Practicing

Once you've watched your surroundings for a long enough period, you'll come to a point when you need to get hands-on and practice. There's no way around practicing if you want to master your purpose deeply. Whatever you want to accomplish, you need fundamentals that you can practice. There's always going to be learning involved with anything new; it's how our brains function.

Before information was easily accessible and written down, humans engaged their mirror neurons to copy their teachers in hands-on practice. The blacksmith didn't have a written recipe guide to build a tool, he taught by verbal instruction, and those learning practiced repetitively. Having information in written form is relatively new (compared to the age of the human race). However, learning by practicing (by doing) has been around far longer; our ancient brains thrive when we learn by doing.

Without being able to learn from hands-on knowledge, wonders such as Machu Picchu would never exist. This wonder exists because of the combined skills of the very resourceful and intelligent Incan race. Even with few tools, Machu Picchu has hundreds of terraces that were (purposely) built using granite, a very tough material. The ancient city has a drainage system that the Incan's built to preserve the structures, and the location exists on a tectonic fault (no accident). The people made the site on the fault because the rocks break along the planes and require less human energy to carve.

Also, thanks to the tectonic fault, water naturally channels directly to the site of Machu Picchu (again, no accident). Finally, the location mitigates avalanches, and only has one way in, which protected the people from invasion. The city is an engineering marvel and one of the most excellent examples of ingenuity and learning through practice and repetition.

Take a hobby such as cooking; we can read a recipe, but it doesn't mean we'll understand how to make it. It's much easier to watch and follow along with someone as they prepare a dish. After we accomplish something, it gets easier the second time, and easier still each time we repeat it. Nobody ever gets worse with practice.

Many times, when we start to practice anything, it's not fun for very long. Initial practices feel like punishments with the repetition, struggle, and no visible progress. However, pushing through this stage of training, we reach the next step, where practice becomes engaging, fun, and we see returns on our efforts. A virtuous cycle forms as we're able to practice longer, which accelerates our learning, further enabling us to keep training and enjoy it.

Always master one skill at a time. Trying to practice five or ten skills will create diminishing returns. The preferred way is to practice one skill to complete mastery. After, choose another skill and practice it until you reach your max ability. Practicing one skill at a time has the bonus effect of enhancing your patience and focus.

Next, accept that the beginning practicing stages will be dull. It's this feeling of dullness that drives most people to quit; however, there's no way around it. The average person is always searching for distractions, a cure for their boredom. Embrace that everything in life does not come instantly, and the highest achievements in life come from practicing long after your mind has told you to quit.

Practice always forms new neural pathways in your brain. Initially, the frontal cortex takes on the task as we learn the activity. Do you know that feeling of intensely focusing on something new? As you repeat it enough, you create connections, and the action gets more comfortable until you can do it without thinking. The neurons we needed in the frontal cortex are available to learn something new, and the process repeats.

Like riding a bicycle, we develop pathways that enable us to return to the task and perform it at the same high level. Can you imagine if you needed to re-practice riding a bike every time you wanted to go for a ride? The deep concentration required to become proficient at anything is the reason we can't try to multitask when we practice. Your goal is to give a single activity your undivided attention for practice.

Understand, it's essential to start your practice in the right way. If you begin to practice the wrong way, all you're doing is learning how to get very good at doing something incorrectly. To start the right way, you need feedback from the right mentors. In the next chapter, we'll do a deep dive into mentors, but for now, you need people who can show you where you are and where you need to go. The people that give you feedback need to be people who have already done what you want to do at the highest levels.

Once you practice enough (correctly), you'll get to a stage where you can start adding your style. You'll begin flowing, the activity will become automatic, and you'll search for what will challenge you further. At this level of skill, it's an extension of you. Many experts suggest that it takes about 10,000 hours of practice to reach this level of proficiency, seven to ten years with a regular practice schedule.

As mentioned, nobody ever gets worse with practice. If you stick with the activity, focus on a single skill, train regularly, and repeat over some years, you'll defeat failure every time.

Phase Three: Testing

When you reach this phase, you've moved from practice to research. You're actively testing new ways with your purpose. For some, this means taking on additional challenges, initiating projects, or opening yourself to constructive feedback from other experts at your level. With testing, you're seeking to uncover any blind spots in your skills. In the first phase (watching), you were keenly observing others; now, you're focused on yourself.

Abraham Lincoln came to a point in his presidency, where he asserted his style by clearly stating his proposals. At the same time, he spoke very plainly, with simple language that everyone understood. President Lincoln was always testing in office as he approached cutting-edge ideas (such as the emancipation proclamation) that stirred strong emotions in the nation.

Michael Jordan was always testing and wanted to know where he was weak. That hunger to understand himself is part of why he watched replays of games and made his practice more difficult. To access this phase, you need to be courageous; when learning something new, many people keep practicing and never start testing their skills. Usually, people are scared to move into testing because they get too comfortable with practice. The practice phase is where people get stuck and start telling themselves they need to improve more before they're ready to take their skills public. The cure for getting past this is to "ready, *fire* aim," jump in and figure it out as you go.

In this testing phase, you're opening yourself up to the criticisms of others. You've learned your purpose at such a skillful level that you're trying new angles and seeing what works. Imagine writing a book; the practice phase would be *writing* the book. Still, the testing phase would be *releasing* it to the public for feedback, digesting the input of others, and writing more.

To be successful and surpass this last phase of learning, you need to be able to take constructive feedback without getting defensive. Through this process, you're learning how to learn correctly. By mastering this process, learning anything will become easy because you'll know what to expect, and you'll be able to identify the phase you're in as you're learning.

Our world has globalized thanks to the rapid expansion of technology. Whatever your purpose is, you'll find that it touches other fields because globalization has brought everything closer together. This global economy means you'll need to be knowledgeable of different areas that affect your interest. For example, finance also involves knowledge of human psychology, nature, and economics. A finance expert is missing pieces of the picture if they don't understand how the brain responds to money.

The future belongs to the prepared, who learn their purpose deeply. For the people that don't value learning, they'll get left behind as the world continues to expand and evolve. Life is a journey of never-ending learning and application; if we stop learning, we start dying.

A word on learning, we live in an academic society. Our culture tends to value academic education more than a practical one. Those that have learned to the point of a Master's or Doctorate are considered the pinnacles of society. On the other hand, those that learned their work through a vocational school, apprenticeship, or on the job training are less meaningful because of the lack of formal education.

Valuing intellect over hands-on experience is a misguided way of thinking. The human race has been around far longer than any university. We thrived before universities by working with our hands and learning by doing. Our ancient brains have a special connection with our hands and our eyes. By working hands-on, we learn to solve issues, develop mechanical thought processes, and practice critical thinking skills. Most importantly, we master putting things into sequences that produce desired results. Look for every opportunity to get hands-on in your practice.

Grandma Moses mastered painting so rapidly, at an advanced age, because all of her practice required hand-eye coordination. To bring your purpose to life, you're taking the intangible, and making it tangible. Your goal starts as nothing more than a thought, a desire, and to bring it to your reality; you need to see yourself as a creator. Before you can bring anything to reality, you must learn the "how," and learning "how" requires you to evolve your skills through practical (hands-on) practice.

The next lessons come from stories of people who have learned their purpose at the deepest level.

Why Education Is More Important Than Money

Robert Kiyosaki, the author of the 1997 best-selling book "Rich Dad Poor Dad," wrote, "there are no good or bad investments, only good or bad investors." How well an investor performs is firmly based on their level of education. In 2008 the United States experienced the most significant housing crash in its history. The biggest losers were the homeowners with little knowledge in real estate, the ones investing for appreciation instead of cash flow.

Millions of people found themselves upside-down because their homes were worth less than they owed on their mortgage. Before the crash, people flooded into the real estate field because of the enormous money to be made. These people chased money, cared less about education, and played a massive part in the crash because of their hunger to earn a commission.

Many *uneducated* people in the financial sector suggested homes to many *ignorant* consumers who weren't creditworthy enough, just to earn a commission off of them. For real estate investors with education, the massive drop in home prices was the most fabulous time of their careers. The educated investors scooped up quality properties, for dirt cheap, from the uneducated people who couldn't pay.

Consequently, the educated investors went on to not only get the appreciation that the uneducated investor desired but also cash flow from renting the property back to ignorant consumers. Ignorant is a strong word to use because good people experienced difficult times during the crash. However, the crash only occurred because money was a higher priority than education.

Unlike education, you can lose money. Knowledge can never be taken and belongs to you for the rest of your life. Even if you lost everything you own, your education could get it all back again. Do you value knowledge or money the most?

When I worked for Quicken Loans in Detroit, I took a mortgage position because the commission brought the *average* worker's pay to $120,000 per year. Nevermind that I knew nothing about real estate, and did the bare minimum to get on the floor and start selling. Education wasn't necessary to me; I cared about commission, titles, and status.

I worked six days per week, averaging 70 hours. Because my thoughts focused on money, I was earning an income that I wasn't ready to have. I didn't have the education to control my success, and I was always on edge, feeling pressure to perform and prove that I deserve the money. All I cared about was myself, and it was affecting my health.

My paycheck was determining what I thought about, the places I went, and what I did with my money. Because I focused entirely on money and not education, my ignorance cost me, and I made decisions that put me in massive debt. Three years later, I'll never forget what it felt like to say to my wife, "we have $15 to get food in the grocery store." That $15 was all I had in my checking account because of my past decisions.

At that moment, I said to myself, "Never again!" I promised that there would never be a moment in mine and my wife's life when we have to try and scrape together food for the week. From that moment forward, my only focus was on educating myself. Because of that decision, I not only paid back the debts from my uneducated (past) self, but I learned to build (and control) a foundation of wealth for my future self and our family.

You'll make effective decisions when you're informed. To become informed, you need to focus your mind on education before money. Choose every opportunity that provides the best learning experiences and chances to work with your hands. Look for opportunities with mentors also focused on knowledge over money. These mentors will be invaluable assets to your success and a constant source of motivation.

Even if you get paid less upfront, don't forget the value of the education you're receiving. Here in Hawaii, many citizens are used to living simple and making it work. The pay for many positions in Hawaii is average compared to the above-average cost of living. Regardless, most locals get creative and live an excellent quality of life with less. One of the skills you need is to learn to do more with less. It's a vital skill because it keeps your mind sharp and resourceful.

Finally, be ready to serve your teachers. Don't ask for anything *from* them, but ask what you can do *for* them. Offer to help them for free without any strings attached. By helping others first, you're setting yourself up. You'll get paid in the form of valuable wisdom, and with it, the money will follow.

Always Reach Up

In 1990, waiting for a train in London, Joanne Rowling imagined a story about a young wizard. Harry Potter was coming to life, but was the world ready?

At the time, Rowling recently graduated from the University of Exeter. Her jobs were temp positions, and she desired to move with her boyfriend in England.

Towards the end of the year, Rowling's mother, Anne, passed away from multiple sclerosis. To cope, Rowling found an English teaching position in Portugal and moved there.

In Porto, The foundation of *Harry Potter* was coming to life in between evening teaching classes and hanging out with roommates. Then, Rowling fell in love with the journalist Jorge Arantes.

Shortly after, Rowling got pregnant and lived with Arantes' mother. Unfortunately, she miscarried. In October 1992, Rowling and Arantes got married and got pregnant again; Rowling gave birth to her baby girl, Jessica, in July.

However, Rowling needed to getaway. Arantes became more abusive, slapped her, and threw her out of their home without her daughter. With assistance, Rowling got her daughter back and was soon heading back to the U.K, carrying the beginning three chapters of Harry Potter.

With little money, Rowling applied for public assistance that helped her get a small place to live and weekly check. Shortly after, she moved to a more welcoming apartment and spent her days writing at her brother-in-law's café with her daughter.

Rowling said that at this time in her life, she was "as poor as it is possible to be in modern Britain, without being homeless." Rowling was feeling a mix of emotions, sadness, anger, and guilt for not giving her daughter the life she deserved.

At one point, Rowling was even considering suicide. However, for her daughter, she chose to reach up, fight, and get things straight in her life. Rowling went through therapy and set the goal of a one-year teaching training course. But, she still had work to do with the young wizard of Hogwarts.

In 1995, Rowling finished the first Harry Potter manuscript. Still, the challenges were only beginning. Rowling reached upward again and sent her manuscript to literary agents. Her three-chapter sample of *Harry Potter* caught the attention of London's Christopher Little. However, the local publishing houses showed little interest in the book.

She got rejected at least a dozen times until her agent found a publisher named Bloomsbury, who offered Rowling a chance. Rowling also got support from the Scottish Arts Council with a grant for her work, enabling her to finish *Harry Potter* with a new typewriter.

On June 26th, 1997, reaching upward was paying off, when *Harry Potter and the Philosopher's Stone* published in the U.K.

Shortly after the publishing, Scholastic (a mega-publisher) bid more than $100,000 for the American publishing rights (The book got renamed to *Harry Potter and The Sorcerer's Stone*). *Harry Potter and the Chamber of Secrets* came a year after, and by 1998, Warner Bros. was ready to make movies. Rowling became the first author billionaire by 2004, fell in love with a Scottish doctor Neil Murray and continued to write best sellers.

J.K. Rowling's story shows that nobody goes out of their way to try to give us a path. As a single mother, Rowling was mostly on her own to succeed. Her story reveals that it took tremendous effort to breakthrough. When she started, she didn't have any high-level connections; she barely had a home at some points.

Nonetheless, Rowling could have accepted starting at the bottom and identified with it. For her daughter, Rowling picked herself up and struggled forward, overcoming numerous obstacles and plenty of rejection. When she showed life, she wouldn't back down, life itself backed down.

Did you notice that Rowling's success improved when the quality of the people around her improved? That was no accident. Our lives always grow when we reach up in our network. Also, her moves to different countries, and various professions, exposed her to multiple cultures, and perspectives, further expanding her horizon. In 2004, the freedom and billionaire success status that Rowling achieved proved that she mastered her highest purpose.

Take A Lesson From Children

Are you familiar with Ryan Wang? Ryan became a pianist when he was four years old. Ryan is only 11 at the time of this writing; however, he's been awarded honors and scholarships from Canadian and international piano competitions. Even more incredibly, he's performed at Carnegie Hall and appeared the Ellen DeGeneres Show.

It doesn't stop there; Ryan received an invitation to represent Canada and perform in the APEC Summit in Beijing, 2014. He also gave the Canadian Prime Minister a private concert. In 2017, Ryan won an Emerging Artist Grant from Vancouver's Academy of Music and participated in Casalmaggiore International Music Festival in Italy; he received first prize at the festival.

In 2017, Ryan toured Southern China, performing in Hong Kong for Radio Hong Kong, Guangzhou, and Xiamen choosing to play Beethoven's Concerto No.1 with Xiamen's Philharmonic orchestra. Then, Ryan got an invitation to perform with the

Singapore Symphony Orchestra for the 100th anniversary dedicated to the Chung Ling High School.

In 2018, Ryan gave a solo in Toronto and played Beethoven's piano concerto No. 2 with Toronto's Festival Orchestra at a New Year's gathering. Then, Ryan got an invitation to be a guest artist with the Vancouver Metropolitan Orchestra as they performed Beethoven's concerto No. 2.

In the middle of 2018, Ryan was the youngest guest to receive an invitation to a program called "Speak to the world." He has performed in many fundraising concerts, supporting Sarah McLachlan's School of Music, the Vancouver hospital, and funding music programs for elementary students in China. At the time of this writing, Ryan Wang is only in the 6th grade.

The lesson to learn from Ryan and other children is that the highest forms of learning come to us when we don't attach ourselves to our beliefs. Kids learn so well because they don't hold onto ideas about *how* things should be. Children's minds are fully open to knowledge; they don't think they're above anything and aren't thinking they know it all.

Learning is simple when we approach it as though we know nothing. The know-it-all who closes their mind also closes themselves off to superior knowledge. When someone is closed off, they're often fearful of change. The confident front is an unconscious defense against having to try something new and risk failure.

Most children's psyches are free of these weaknesses. Children have a long cycle of needing to be taken care of; they're used to feeling a dependency on adults. Because they rely on others, children desire to learn and feel independent. Kids soak up information quickly, they don't block their progress, and they master what they love.

No matter your age, think about what you loved as a child. You can always unleash your childlike spirit, find wonder in the world, and choose to learn without any preconceived notions. Whatever new venture you immerse yourself in, take yourself back to those feelings of being a child. Learn with a completely open mind and heart. Treat others as though they are the experts who hold the keys to learning and fulfilling your highest purpose.

You're looking to find a constant feeling of curiosity. Let go of fears, superiority, assumptions, and preconceived notions. You are choosing to defer to other people and keep an openness to learning so that in the future, you will master learning your purpose (like Ryan Wang) and liberate yourself.

Have Faith

"Enter by the narrow gate. For the gate is wide and the way is easy that leads to destruction, and those who enter by it are many. For the gate is narrow and the way is hard that leads to life,

and those who find it are few." - Matthew 7:14 ESV

When we learn new skills, it's tempting to look for the easy way around the process. Many people get to the point of irritation because they don't see the progress they expect. Initial enthusiasm can fade, and what's left is repetition, practice, and boredom with no guarantee of results. By listening to our minds telling us to quit, we drift away from what we're pursuing, never reaching our full potential.

When we don't finish something, it means we have more faith in that voice in our head than the process. Frustration fuels the voice in our head, and when we don't push well past it, we never see results. When you were young, when was a time you were frustrated but kept going and succeeded? When you're having difficulty in the present, think back to a time when you felt the same, pushed forward (on faith), and experienced a breakthrough.

Nobody achieves their highest purpose without devoting time to the process. As you push forward, days pass, then weeks, then months, and years until that day that you breakthrough. Once you master a skill, it's yours, and the most beautiful gift you can receive because you earned it. Regardless of where you start, the formula to a breakthrough requires practice, time, and faith.

Frustration and irritation will present themselves every time you start learning something new. We all experience those feelings, and you'll need to embrace them. If you're not irritated, you're not growing. The irritation is your signal that your mind is working on mastering the information you're giving it, and you require more time and practice. Have faith that you'll continue to progress every time you show up, and your success will come; nobody has ever gotten worse with repeated practice.

As mentioned, people like to take the wide gate, the most convenient way on their path. This analogy means that these are the ones that aren't willing to practice once they find their purpose. It might be an easy gate, but it leads to a difficult life.

The narrow gate is uncomfortable, it's frustrating, and it takes effort. Those that choose the narrow gate are committing to challenging themselves. Ironically, with those challenges, people live an easier and more fulfilling life.

Few find the narrow gate because they don't want to search for it. By searching for the narrow gate, you're searching for your purpose. When you find it, then you have to overcome the learning process (the gatekeeper). However, to pass through that narrow gate is to pass through to the most significant feeling of satisfaction and meaning that a person can attain. The mastery of your purpose allows you to bless others and help them move through their narrow gate. Giving this to others is the height of fulfillment.

Choosing The Narrow Gate

We have a preference for that which is comfortable (easy). If someone can get the same result with less effort, why put themselves through pain? Many people don't want to work and are willing to take social security or welfare because it's easier. Even with a lower quality of life, many choose to take the handout because it's a "free lunch."

Taking this route is the way of the weak. To master your purpose, you must add additional pressure to your practice. To begin, ignore that voice in your head that wants what's comfortable. Create a habit of putting yourself in uncomfortable situations that challenge you. Find the satisfaction that comes with knowing that temporary discomfort makes for a healthy life.

Next, focus intensely. When you're practicing your purpose, don't scatter your attention. Your practice is sacred time, free of interruptions and distractions. Your training sessions are also intense, make them more difficult for yourself, so the skills are rooted deep in your central nervous system. When you slay the "biggest" dragons, you've conquered the most significant challenges, and everything after that feels simple.

Like Michael Jordan, use your imagination to create challenges and set made-up standards for yourself. Consciously choose the rules for your life and ensure you set a higher bar for yourself than others. A few hours of intense practice under these conditions will forge you under pressure. You'll soon excel in your purpose, and execute it with ease. In seeing your level of achievement, other people will give you more freedom because humans are inclined to defer to those perceived as experts.

Failure Is A Blessing

The Disney company we know today had an incredibly challenging start. Walt Disney failed in multiple businesses, had countless setbacks, and grew up poor under the household of the violent Elias Disney (his father). Since a young age, Walt's escape was to draw. As the second youngest sibling, Walt grew up seeing his siblings run away from their father. Walt escaped by getting a job driving an ambulance in WW1 before he was old enough.

    When Walt returned from WW1, he and his brother Roy Disney started a cartoon studio called "Laugh-O-Gram Studios," which went bankrupt shortly after forming. With almost no money, Disney headed west to California, took up a brief stint in acting, and failed again.

    However, California had very little competition in animation at the time. So, Walt invited Roy to join him and start another business. This time, Disney struck gold with Oswald The Lucky Rabbit. At the time, Oswald was in one-reel animations, and kind of resembled Mickey Mouse if Mickey was a rabbit. However, Oswald and Disney would face trouble soon after.

    In a power play, Disney's producer in New York grabbed Oswald's animators, ensuring that Walt no longer had legal rights to Oswald. Without a hassle, Disney gave up Oswald, but Mickey Mouse was born on the trip back to California. The Mickey Mouse we know and love was a complete failure at the start.

Walt accumulated massive debt and could barely afford food. A few hundred financers reportedly turned down Mickey. Walt Disney was heading towards depression as he struggled to keep his business alive and got yet another crucial employee stolen from him. Disney recovered powerfully, as you're about to see.

The year is 1937, and Disney's first animation feature film was released. It was a *little* title called "Snow White and the Seven Dwarfs." The film was a sensational hit in the box offices. Unfortunately, his three movies to follow, Pinnochio, Fantasia, and Bambi, fell flat.

Around the start of World War II, Disney's debts were pushing about $4 million. His animation team was striking, and film studios were putting pressure on Disney to stay in the box office instead of moving to television. The move to T.V. paid off, between Davy Crockett and The Mickey Mouse Club Disney controlled enough capital for the makings of Disneyland.

Is this where Disney got him happily ever after? Not even close. Aside from the massive capital outlay that Disneyland required, and some very close calls with bankruptcy (again), Disneyland opened on July 17th, 1955. People remember that day as "Black Sunday." It was crowded, hot, people were forging tickets, rides and drinking fountains were breaking, and the line to get in was roughly seven miles.

As you know, Walt Disney and his empire succeeded through grit and perseverance. Here's what he thought about failure:

Walt Disney's Guidance

"All the adversity I've had in my life, all the troubles and obstacles,

> *have strengthened me. You may not realize it when it happens, but a kick in the teeth may be the best thing in the world for you"* –
> Walt Disney

Failure is a blessing that can feel like a curse. By failing, you've learned what doesn't work. Knowing what doesn't work enables you to try a different route. Walt Disney's path had adversity, but he kept going, and going, and going. Look at his empire now. That buildup of failures he faced exploded into a legacy of tremendous success.

Failure is just your education. Where most people are too friendly to hurt your feelings and tell you where you need to improve, failure is blunt. Failure doesn't discriminate; it is just the gatekeeper that will reward or deny you access to success.

Failure comes from either not trying, or (like Walt) trying. The former is a failure that provides nothing. The latter challenges people with adversity but rewards them with knowledge, skills, and success. Getting a lucky break from the beginning is the worst thing that can happen to you. It dulls the mind, elevates the ego, and provides undeserved rewards. The best path is failing our way to success. In this way, we not only get the achievements we desire, but we gain an unbreakable spirit and wisdom that nobody can take from us.

Take action on your ideas, open yourself to public criticism, fail beautifully, learn, and always come back for another round.

Understand Your Surroundings

Our eyes can deceive us. Einstein was famous for the theories of general and special relativity. The theory of general relativity is one of gravity. In contrast, special relativity explains how an object moving at the speed of light cannot travel quicker than light.

These theories are relevant because everything in life has a world of the *seen* and the *unseen*. Just because something we can see, doesn't mean we can necessarily see it with our eyes. We have always known that there's this invisible force called gravity, and even though it's hidden, we can see that something is keeping objects on the ground. However, did we understand *how* gravity works?

Alternatively, we know that light travels at 299,792 kilometers per second. While we can see a range of colors, we can't see them all because of their different wavelengths; colors of light are seen or unseen.

The vital point is that to get a full picture of our surroundings, we need to understand *what* is around us and *how* it works. If we only see *what* is around us, we're letting our eyes dictate what we believe is reality. But, when we combine what we *see* with an understanding of *how* things work, we move closer to reality.

Grasping *how* things work is less exciting because it often requires the use of imagination. For instance, we drive cars, but we may or may not know how the car comes together to produce a complete product. We order a product from Amazon, but don't see the business systems and processes used to create, package, and ship it (the how).

By seeking to understand the unseen behind the seen, Einstein gained a much more in-depth knowledge of mass and energy. A level of expertise so deep that he triumphed over fundamental physics with his equation, $E=mc^2$. The combination of the seen and unseen brought Einstein closer to reality, challenged the truth of what people thought they knew and left the human race better for it.

Our world remains divided between those that consume without an understanding and those that want to understand. With the infinite information available to us, choose to learn how the things in your environment work. This understanding includes processes, people, mechanics, technology, and anything that's directly vital to your highest purpose.

Always ask "how" questions: How does that function? How was that made? How was this team - formed? Understanding what is unseen will bring you closer to the truths of life. When you move towards truth, like Einstein, you can change reality.

Try And Try Again

Do you know why Amazon is a billion-dollar giant? Because they're willing to innovate and make mistakes that cost billions. In 2016, Jeff Bezos called Amazon "the best place in the world to fail." Every innovative idea that Bezos has acted on came with some risk. Let's take a glimpse at the errors that have molded Amazon's success.

Let's begin with Amazon Spark. It featured the product in photos, similar to a visual Instagram shopping experience. The idea flopped, and Amazon has since pivoted the idea to a page called #FoundItOnAmazon.

Did you know that Amazon used to deliver food from restaurants using their same-day delivery service? It was a GrubHub kind of service called Amazon Restaurants. The service launched in 2015 and stopped a few years later.

Amazon also had a service called Amazon Storywriter and Amazon Storybuilder. The premise of the service was that aspiring screenwriters could submit their film ideas to Amazon for consideration; as of 2018, Amazon stopped accepting scripts.

Did you ever visit an Amazon pop-up store while they were a thing? Did you know that Amazon had 87 kiosks that they started to enable consumers to try Echo and Fire T.V. offerings before purchasing them? The company chose to shut them down and focus on Amazon books instead.

The next one was very innovative. What if you had a button that you could mount in a convenient place and press whenever you needed a refill of an item? Say, a button next to the toilet paper dispenser that automatically orders toilet paper? Amazon tried it, and it was called the dash button. The goal was for consumables to get replenished automatically, but Amazon didn't consider how many consumables a home can contain. So, they never conceived that the house could have a ton of buttons everywhere. Dash buttons were only successful in getting consumers to shop without a screen.

Before the ultra-popular Amazon Echo, there was the tap. The tap was a mobile-version of Alexa. It was battery-operated and designed to be a portable solution. It got replaced by Alexa and became available in a certified refurbished form only. Amazon (wisely) transitioned to an "Alexa everywhere" strategy, putting their Alexa voice assistant into all of their products.

In 2018, Amazon discontinued a pickup service where consumers could visit a designated site, and use a barcode to get the product they purchased. Let's say you order a snack and want it within minutes. An Amazon employee would fill a designated locker with your item, and you'd go into the site and pick it up.

There was no confirmation when the service discontinued, but if it worked, it would still be around.

Did you ever buy tickets from Amazon tickets? Well, if you missed the boat, so did most. Amazon tickets were an innovative ticketing service that Amazon began testing in 2015. Of course, by 2018, the service was canceled. There was some talk about a new ticketing program launching in 2019, but Ticketmaster still reigns supreme.

Next, we move to groceries. Amazon purchased Whole Foods, but they didn't take-off with their Whole Foods 365 program. The program's original conception was to be a budget-friendly alternative for younger shoppers. The idea failed because of the pricing difference between the 365 brand and the Whole Foods stores.

Staying with the grocery store theme, Amazon tested out "Amazon Fresh." It was to be a grocery-delivery service, and it was Amazon's competitive answer to a company called Peapod. The difference is that Peapod has their system figured out, while Amazon didn't have a supply chain in place that enabled them to compete.

The list could go on from payment services to vacations, to websites, and local initiatives. The takeaway is that Amazon progresses forward because of its trial and error. As of this writing, Amazon is worth over $1 trillion.

Unlike previous generations, we create new ways of operating that suit the time. The boomer generation valued choosing a career and building seniority within that field. Subsequent generations value freedom, mobility, and the use of technology to accomplish their goals. Information is abundant, and we're easily able to use trial and error to see what works for us uniquely. You can learn anything openly, unlike any other time in history,

By gaining a firm understanding of your surroundings, you build confidence to take advantage of the opportunities that will show themselves to you.

Your knowledge will allow you to act on those opportunities, and you'll be able to combine different schools of learning to produce different results.

You don't need to follow a specific "career path" like previous generations. Once you understand your purpose, you can branch into different disciplines of knowledge and learn them. The people whose goal is to "climb the ladder" end up old and frustrated.

Part II

Chapter 3: Choose Your Mentor

We all have limited time, and trying to learn without guidance can steal years of your life in wasted productivity. The quickest way to get what you want is to learn from a mentor who already has it. The right teacher will challenge you, guide you, and give you access to their experience. Mentors provide realtime feedback that saves you years and improves your skills quickly.

Most importantly, behavior and emotions are contagious. You will adopt your mentor's way of approaching success and failure. Over time, your personality will show itself in your purpose. You'll take your teacher's advice that works for you, you'll drop what doesn't, and you'll progress your field.

The mentor you choose needs to be one that aligns with your goals and your purpose. As mentioned, you will come to a time when you need to spread your wings and break free from your teacher. At that level, you'll rival and potentially surpass your teacher, just as your teacher surpassed his mentors.

Tony Robbins Mentor

Tony Robbins grew up in an environment that was less than supportive. He didn't have a father figure as a child, and his mom wrestled with substance abuse. To get away, Tony read books regularly. Robbins openly admitted that he used books to get his mentorship. Tony often read biographies of the most successful figures of the time, learning how they turned their suffering into success. Through books, Robbins began looking at the world in new ways.

Robbin's first real teacher (that wasn't a book), was a motivational force named Jim Rohn. One of Tony's significant changes in thought came when Rohn told him:

Jim Rohn's Guidance

"If you want anything to change, you must change, and if you want things to get better, you've got to get better." – Jim Rohn

Rohn showed Robbins that once he *commits* to higher standards for himself, he'll have more to give other people. This one person empowered Tony's love for knowledge and gave him the successful model he desired. Although Rohn passed away in 2009, Robbins said, "His spirit and mentorship continues to live on in me and through so many others shaped by his wisdom."

But Rohn was just the first mentor. Possibilities began opening up in Tony's life, and he met more mentors along his journey that shaped his philosophies. A crucial lesson to remember is that each mentor has unique strengths for you to learn. So, you might have a mentor for your spirit, your body, your finances, your mind, and more. Several mentors will give you a diverse perspective, complement, and enhance your personality.

Robbin's next mentor was the founder of the neuro-linguistic programming (NLP) movement. NLP used mind and behavior to achieve goals and overcome barriers. In essence, this mentor taught Tony that the state of our mind correlates to the state of our body. The teacher's name is John Grinder.

One of Grinder's crucial lessons was that people who get results leave clues. It's unnecessary to reinvent the wheel; you simply have to model precisely what someone successful is already doing. By modeling success, you automatically put yourself on the path to get the same outcome.

Grinder showed Robbins how essential health is for lasting success. Tony learned that he could change his perspective and quality of life just by changing his physiology. For example, changing from sitting to standing, or standing to walking, or walking to jogging. And that we will only go as far as our bodies let us go, thus the importance of making health a lifestyle choice.

After Grinder, Robbins met a creative force named Peter Guber. This mentor's strength was moving people through telling stories. Guber mentored Robbins on bringing out everyone's best story. Because we all tell ourselves stories, we can choose to change it at any moment. The first step, as Guber described, is to be genuinely interested in others; it's expressing care for the wellbeing of others.

Next, Guber taught that generosity is crucial. The kind of generosity where we make others aware of their strengths and help them harness it to enhance their quality of life. To help people craft a new story, both parties have to exchange in dialogue. Instead of one person telling the other what to do, the process is interactive, and you're helping people take ownership of their best selves.

Robbin's mentorship with Guber is a give and take, symbiotic kind of relationship. Guber doesn't always play the mentor; sometimes, he defers to the wisdom of Robbin's and vice versa. This relationship taught Tony the importance of being service-minded to things more significant than any individual. Even more, it taught him that living means giving and that a cornerstone of successful people is what they contribute to others.

Remember, mentors give you things that you'll never get by reading books or searching on Youtube. So, what is Tony Robbin's suggestion for finding your mentor?

Tony Robbin's Guidance

"The secret to massively accelerating the quality of your life is to learn from the people that you find to be the teachers and, more importantly, the doers in the world. Many people talk: my advice is to model the few who don't just talk but actually do. It's an open opportunity to benefit from their successes and their failures."

How To Make The Most Of Mentoring

When you initially learn from mentors, your role is to serve them. When it comes to your purpose, see yourself as knowing nothing, and defer to their wisdom. Later in the mentorship, as you elevate your skills, you will reach a point of creativity where you challenge the ways of your teachers, and set your unique path. Until then, you need their guidance. The following wisdom will help you get the most value from your mentors.

First, choose people that align with your most significant desires. The people you learn from must have what you want already. People that want to help you, but have no experience, cannot get you results. Everyone has an opinion, but far fewer people have the wisdom you need.

Bill Gates always hovers around the top 5 for the world's wealthiest people. At that level, some might think that Gates doesn't need a mentor. However, Gates has a mentor. Can you guess who? It's fellow billionaire Warren Buffett. Although Gates and Buffett are close friends, Gates admits that he defers to Buffett's wisdom often; Buffett also had a mentor in the late investor Benjamin Graham.

The mentors we choose are critical. Also, the relationship you have with your mentor is vital. Buffett and Gates have a mentorship with reciprocity. Sometimes Buffett is the mentor, and sometimes its Gates. If the relationship wasn't balanced, Gates might have never broken away from the style of his mentor. Gates could have become a copy of Buffett, never expressing his unique personality.

Common mistakes in choosing teachers are to pick the person that seems the smartest, the one who has the most recognition or is the nicest. The choice requires detailed analysis, keeping your goals and passions in mind. Can the person help you become your ideal future-self? Your mentor needs to match your temperament.

It's ok if you don't know your purpose or direction because your mentors can enlighten your path. Consider teachers who have differing views than you. Different perspectives promote growth, and sometimes teachers can challenge us in areas that we want to avoid.

Mentorship is a lot like a family. Our families exist to guide us to the best of their ability. We don't always agree with them, they challenge us and frustrate us, but we take lessons from them. The lessons may be what to do or what *not* to do. Still, unlike family, you can choose your mentors. Most importantly, teachers can provide you the qualities that your family didn't give you. Be careful to avoid selecting mentors that feel familiar, or you'll repeat mistakes.

Second, choose mentors who tell things as they are. In Ray Dalio's book, Principles, Dalio says that "Pain + Reflection = progress." Reaching your highest purpose will require courage, toughness, and getting to the truth of events. Dalio suggests that it's vital to make decisions according to the principles of reality.

Without mentors, it's challenging to push ourselves and identify where we're weak. It's the pressure of difficult situations that forces our most significant growth. Still, we live in an age that is less challenging than at any time in recorded human history. Many people are polite, yet dishonest, unwilling to tell people the truth about their situation. We sacrifice growth because we don't want people to show us things that go against our ego's.

    The people that don't tell us what we need to hear, flatter us, and hold us back from reaching our potential. As Dalio suggests, we need constructive criticism that brings us closer to reality. With facts, we gain discipline and improve our willpower to master our highest purpose. Those that have succeeded in your mission understand the pain and setbacks it took to get there. So, they can identify where you are in your path, and empathize with your challenges. You need tough love, and you need people who will show you the reality of who you are. When you live in the truth of who you are, you develop a different, elevated form of confidence that is unbreakable.

Third, try everything and differentiate yourself. We face a delicate balance when being mentored. We need to learn from others, but by following them too closely, we can forfeit the uniqueness we bring to our purpose. The artist will never be successful if they rigidly follow form. However, an artist without the right foundation will not produce professional work.

The solution is to try everything you learn from your mentors, and only keep that which aligns with your personality. At the beginning of your learning process, you will most likely need to copy your teacher's style. Although, with practice, you will reach a level of skill where you feel the urge to be creative. Don't resist the urge to inject creativity into your purpose. If you don't add your personality, your work will never reach the heights of your capabilities.

Johann Ambrosius Bach (1645–1695) was the father of the famous Johann Sebastian Bach. The former was a talented violinist who taught his son how to play. However, Johann Ambrosius Bach passed away when his son was only 10. Shortly after, Bach's older brother

Johann Christoph took care of him and provided further musical instruction until he was 15 years old.

As we know, Johann Sebastian went on to have an illustrious career, heavily influenced by his Lutheran faith. Still, Bach developed his style by learning from his father and brother (mentors) and eventually reaching a level of skill where he applied his personality to his work. Although Bach had a large family, and a long line of musical heritage, his name stands as the most prominent of all.

No one would likely know the brilliance of Johann Sebastian had he not adopted the best parts of what he learned, and discarded others. Bach's philosophy was this:

Johann Sebastian Bach's Guidance

"I play the notes as they are written, but it is God who makes

the music."
— Johann Sebastian Bach

What Bach is suggesting is that he learned to play the notes as instructed. However, his inspiration (God) turned the notes into music. For your life's purpose, you need to let your mentors teach you how to "play." But, once you learn, if you allow your inspiration to express itself, you won't just play, you will create "music."

Slowly create distance between you and your mentor, realize that their teachings are adaptable to your situation, and seek to surpass them. As Bach surpassed the prowess of his siblings, so to should you move beyond your teachers. Your teachers followed the same process surpassing their mentors, and so on. Whatever your purpose is, remember that you are evolving the field of study and positively contributing to humanity.

Fourth, the mentor-mentee relationship needs to be a give and take. Teachers aren't always teaching; they can learn from those that they mentor. At times in the relationship, mentees can lend their strengths to mentors.

The U.S. Army challenged my spirit more than any other period in life. A friend of mine started as my leadership and set me up for massive success. His most admirable quality is that he expresses willingness to learn, just as he expresses a desire to lead others. Thanks to his dedication to mentorship, I left the Army more decorated than all of the soldiers around me.

However, because of my passion for investing and entrepreneurship, he also developed a love for financial education and made significant returns on his investments. Can you imagine if he decided to ignore me because I was the mentee? He could have missed massive opportunities for me to serve him with my strengths.

Unlike most people, he never let his ego get the best of him because of military rank. Many of his prior colleagues are still breaking their backs in the military. At the same time, he finished his service with an abundance of passive income. Because of his guidance, I was able to avoid numerous pitfalls, get into the shape of my life, and fast-track a couple of ranks before getting out.

Many mentor-mentee relationships can become stale unless we consciously maintain our engagement from start to finish. Often, when the relationship starts falling apart, it's because one party starts to treat the other differently. Maybe the mentor is beginning to feel threatened by the mentee, or perhaps the mentee feels like they can't escape the shadow of their mentor.

Either way, as the mentee grows, they will shed the principles of the mentor that don't work for them. When they start to branch off a different way, they're no longer as similar to their teacher as they used to be. Even more, the teacher might feel that his student is threatening their cherished principles. The solution is to develop a bond of giving and taking.

My friend and I have a dynamic mentorship because we have both adopted some of each other's ideas. Because both of us have said yes to each other's thoughts, the relationship never gets stale, and we have demonstrated our willingness to learn from one another. In mutually accepting wisdom from our experiences, our minds remain fluid; we never get stuck in our ways.

Similar to when I met my mentor, you must express respect and devote all of your attention to learning. You are a sponge, show your teachers how well you absorb their wisdom. My mentor was willing to listen to me because I first listened to him. When you give all of your attention, you learn more quickly, grow, and contribute ideas back to your mentor.

But, it all begins with a desire to learn, your approach to mentorship, and creating an environment of reciprocity.

Chapter 4: Build Your Identity

Your peers are one significant challenge to building an identity around your purpose. People can steer us in the wrong direction, stand in the way of progress, and have hidden agendas. What people say is not always what they mean, and our reactions can get lost in translation and strain relationships.

As you build your new identity, you need to have an acute sense of observing people's actions in reality. By seamlessly navigating the social aspect of our lives, we free ourselves to focus on absorbing knowledge and taking action towards our purpose. Without an ability to read others, your highest mission can never happen because you need people to get what you want. And, people help people that they like.

Nelson Mandela

At age 16, Nelson Mandela began building his identity around his political purpose. In his culture, 16-year-old boys participated in an African circumcision ritual. The ritual was considered the passage to become a man. For context, a man who did not get circumcised was not allowed to inherit wealth, be an officiant at tribal rituals, or get married.

Mandela and 25 boys participated, but he was changed when the officiant of the ceremony, Chief Meligqili, expressed sadness for Mandela and his peers. The chief explained that they would not have any governing power due to white men's control in their country. Furthermore, the 25 boys would never reach their full potential because their destiny was to do worthless work for white men.

Mandela admitted that he didn't fully grasp the chief's words that day. However, it planted the seed to help push him towards his vision of a liberated South Africa. In 1942, Mandela joined a group called the African National Congress, whose purpose was to support the anti-apartheid movement. The goal was to empower the working people to take action against the current government.

In the first decade, Mandela staged protests against government policies, but by 1961 everything changed. For organizing a strike of working citizens, Mandela got arrested and sentenced to 5 years in prison. By 1963, Mandela was back in court, facing a life sentence for sabotage and other political crimes.

1963 was the beginning of 27 years in prison. Mandela built his identity from behind prison bars, even earning his law degree. All of his effort and suffering to one day see his vision of a free South Africa. As time passed, Mandela's power grew, sparking an international protest for his release. His break came when President Botha passed away. His replacement, a more supportive Frederik Willem de Klerk, lifted the African National Congress ban and announced Mandela's release amid growing international demand.

Upon release, Mandela immediately embodied the identity of a political leader who demanded reform from the South African government. Just three years after his release in 1990, Mandela won the Nobel Peace Prize for his work against apartheid in South Africa. Still, only a year after, successful negotiations between black and white South Africans lead to the first democratic presidential election. At 77 years old, Nelson Mandela became the first black president in the history of South Africa.

Nelson Mandela's Guidance

> *"One of the things I learned when I was negotiating was that until I changed myself, I could not change others."*
> — Nelson Mandela

To successfully navigate the social aspect of armed resistance and protests, Mandela kept a balance of political pressure while negotiating for the end of apartheid. Upon release, he knew he needed to leave his hatred and bitterness at the prison door, or he would end up locked up again. So, with social intelligence, Mandela navigated delicate negotiations to end apartheid.

The most significant change in Mandela's life was how he matured in prison. He went into prison with a certain mindset. But, once released, his social intelligence had blossomed to the point where he was ready to lead his country to freedom. What this means is that Mandela deeply understood people.

Apartheid could never have ended without adopting a different perspective about people. In building your identity, your social intelligence needs refining. We can all improve ourselves in this aspect when we shed our old ways of being. Reflect on your history, when were you caught in battles with other people? When were you not getting what you want?

Don't focus on people's actions towards you, but ask yourself, how did you view those people? What labels did you assign to them? Were there warning signs about them that were ignored or missed? Your goal is to get to the reality of every situation. Who did you believe those people were? Consider how you helped to fuel the problem.

We don't always know people's true intentions, so we have to observe them, instead of reacting. We were all ignorant at one point; we were raised with false beliefs about the world from people (parents and peers) because we adopted thoughts from them. Accept that some people have poor qualities and can act in ways that hurt others.

Patiently watch people, take note of their actions, and you'll be able to understand and persuade them as needed. Through your observations, you'll notice that there are two types of knowledge you need to navigate social interactions.

First, you need to excel at being able to understand people, their thoughts of the world, and their unique personality. Second, you need to study the macro (general) behaviors of people, as well as the negative behaviors that some people possess. When you understand individual, as well as general human behaviors, you'll have the keys to making intelligent social decisions based on reality. These skills need to be a part of the identity you build, so we'll talk about each of the two components in turn.

Understanding Individual Behaviors

Let's start with understanding individual behaviors. Before the invention of language, our ancient ancestors still needed to communicate. As a result, they became extraordinary at understanding non-verbal communication. Our brains are old mechanisms that still have the makings of those that came before us.

Think about a person you feel comfortable around. Are you nervous speaking with them? Are you focused on what you'll say next? Of course not, because you're not focusing on yourself; you're focusing outward. Contrast that with a first date. Two people meet, they're nervous, inwardly focused on what to say, neither person starts out expressing deep emotions.

However, when there's a connection between two people, communication flows with no effort. The most important parts of the interaction are non-verbal, such as body language and vocal tonality. In those moments, we're using parts of our brain derived from our ancestors. In our heightened state, we effectively observe people.

To understand people, always look at their non-verbal behaviors instead of their verbal. You'll learn everything from body language, tone of voice, and eye contact. In an emotional state, people will further show their real character to you. But, to do this effectively, you need to focus outside of yourself. Getting caught up in your internal dialogue will cause you to miss vital social cues.

When you focus on others, they will make you feel specific ways. Have faith in your feelings. Your feelings will be your queue on how to proceed. Upon reflection, you can analyze your feelings in these moments and choose what you define them as.

Consider the nervousness that most people reveal when they're in the presence of someone with a prominent title or rank. Many will show signs of anxiety, discomfort, or jealousy, often submitting to the other person's perceived power.

Imagine this, if you had grown up in another person's shoes, lived through their childhood, with their parents and peers, wouldn't you act the same way they do? Try to connect with them on common ground, imagine how they feel, and feel an emotion that they do. This emotional similarity will build instant rapport between you and others because you'll connect with a deeper understanding of them.

Have fun with this, and imagine yourself switching minds with others. Getting into the headspace of others is an effective way to make your thoughts more open and fluid. Also, you're flexing your creative muscles, which will only improve as you use them more.

It was once said to pay attention to how a person treats their server at a restaurant. Someone kind to you, but mean to their server, is, in reality, a mean person. Before investing with anyone, I prefer to meet at their home. People can fake themselves, but animals can't. So, I meet at their house so I can meet their animals. If their animals are kind, I'm confident that I'm dealing with a kind person. However, if their animals are aggressive, likely, the person isn't who they appear to be.

Next, watch for any extreme qualities in people. When someone expresses an extreme behavior, they are likely the opposite of that behavior. Overly confident people tend to be insecure, excessively kind people tend to be aggressive, and so on. Also, observe people's environment. T. Harv Eker, best selling author or Secrets Of The Millionaire Mind, once said, how people do anything is how they do everything. Every detail of other people matters.

Finally, instead of relying on intuition or your first impression of a person, give yourself space and time to observe their character. Most people have an initial persona, and only over time will their real personality reveal itself. Realize, once you deeply understand another person's behavior, it doesn't mean that their character will stay the same. Understanding people is a constant process of observing behavior and remaining open-minded.

General Human Behaviors

Let's next understand general behaviors people can have. People have some general qualities that span cultural boundaries. These qualities are uniquely human and exist universally. For example, a positive human quality is our ability to work as a team to accomplish goals. However, we also have undesirable attributes that require discussion.

Jealousy is the first general behavior. We have a long history of comparing ourselves to people around us. At times, it can seem that everyone else has life figured out. But don't let what you see deceive you. Living with jealousy gives other people undeserved attention. When our envy penetrates us deep enough, we feel the desire to stand in the way of the people who remind us of the emotion.

Watch for the people who overly celebrate you. The unusually friendly people may likely hold some jealousy, and seek to stop your progress. Also, read people for insecure, even passive-aggressive behavior, which suggests they might hold jealous feelings. Envy triggers from arrogant displays of your strength, which makes others feel inadequate about themselves.

To ensure people don't become jealous of you, demonstrate your weaknesses to others, or show interest in people by making them feel included and validated. Also, never talk above people and make them feel unintelligent in your presence. Many people get jealous when they feel less intelligent than others around them.

Don't make yourself a target of jealousy by standing out. Match your surroundings like a chameleon, make others feel like you're one of them. Seek to master your purpose and reach a level of success where the people around you can no longer bring you down.

Groupthink is the next general behavior. When groups form, they're a double-edged sword. The diversity of a group is a powerful tool to solve challenges and achieve goals. Although, that diversity comes at the price of groupthink.

People in groups quickly establish hierarchies and chains of command, even if nobody formally acknowledges it. You'll notice the many in the group adopt the beliefs of the group leaders. Afraid to stand out, they go along with the crowd, so they don't seem different, like less of a team player.

You are different because you want to achieve your highest purpose. Until you gain power in your environment, take care not to express too many differences with groups. Your expression of your individuality comes from the work you accomplish. However, when you have to play politics in your environment, heir on the side of being agreeable, even if you don't entirely agree. You will need people around you to help you in achieving your goals.

The people who ignore groupthink and try to show too much individual character draw negative attention towards themselves. Others will not want to associate themselves with people who can't be agreeable; they will shun the individual from the group. Keep in mind that when you reach heights of success, you will be free to express your real nature because you will become that person that the group considers their leader.

Vanity is the third general human behavior. We default to thinking about our self-interests before others. With the increasing competitiveness of the world, we concern ourselves with how we will get our share. Even when we take seemingly selfless actions, it's because we're concerned with how we will look. There is nothing wrong with this behavior. However, openly expressing our self-interest to others isn't attractive, so many people will disguise it.

Consider the opposite; if a person has a high degree of self-interest, they usually *seem* to be the most giving and selfless. These people will show support for causes, and seem to have a spirit of goodness. But, you'll see their real behavior when you request something from them. The people who put up a false front are frustrating because they won't be congruent with who they seem to be, they'll refuse to help you, or avoid your requests.

The core reason these people don't help you is that they aren't selfless people. They deny or avoid you because they can't see what's in it for them. To effectively navigate this human behavior, start by showing people what they get. Consider what they need, something that is highly valuable, and deliver it to them.

When you request anything from people, frame the request this way: "If I do **X** for you, would you do **Y** for me?" What benefit can you deliver that will excite them? Be interested in them, more than trying to be involved in yourself. Approaching people in this way will ensure people say *yes* to you more often than not.

Stubbornness is next. Technology rapidly expands our world and creates constant changes. The challenge is that many people want life to remain static, so they cling to things that make them feel comfortable. It's soothing to know what to expect and uncomfortable to face the unexpected. The general response is to hold onto the old or try to take things "back to the basics."

Take microwaves; for example, they came into existence in 1946 but didn't start gaining high acceptance in homes until 1967. The technology had more skeptics than believers, and it had to be the early adopters that helped skeptics past their stubbornness.

It took from 1950 – 1975 for sales of the microwave to increase 10x from 10,000 to 100,000. Also, it took until the mid-1980s to reach 5 million sales. Nonetheless, today microwaves are in over 90% of homes in the United States.

The microwave continues to be a staple in households, which most people never think twice about using. Although, there was a time skeptics fought to keep things as they were. To accept the microwave was to think differently, and many people could not bring themselves to adapt. Nobody goes around proudly marketing that they're a stubborn person. However, you will see this behavior come out in some when you introduce newness.

Unfortunately, not even logic and reality can persuade these people against their stubborn thoughts. This behavior is critical to understand because you can inadvertently make enemies by changing the fragile order in their lives. The only solution is to accept that some people have this behavior. Take it as a lesson, and reminder, to keep your mind fluid and open to new thoughts.

Passive-aggression is the 5th behavior to keep on your radar. People who have this tendency are scared of the emotional turmoil that can arise from confronting problems directly. Being passive-aggressive comes from a need to control outcomes. Still, we are each passive-aggressive to some level.

Consider some of the common examples, such as being chronically late, or making side comments towards others. To effectively deal with this passive aggression, there are only two options; you can bring it to the persons' attention or not respond. Be careful with these types of people; they're highly charged with passive aggression because they are also highly insecure.

This behavior is why it's vital to understand human behavior. People can use passive aggression to fly under the radar and quietly ruin lives. The best offense against this behavior is to distance yourself from the start. Consider this, does the person have a history of this behavior? Have others fallen victim to them? Who's around them the most often? Are those people often guarded, cautious, or anxious?

Watch for the opposite behavior. Passive-aggressive people don't often advertise it. The best method to see people's real persona is to note their *actions*. Stay out of these people's drama; nothing good comes from going back and forth with a passive-aggressive personality; it's a losing battle.

The takeaway from these individual and general human behaviors is that you're effectively managing relationships in your network. Also, understanding these behaviors allows you to keep your thoughts clear, so nothing takes you away from your highest purpose. Take the story of Nelson Mandela; he used his social intelligence to bridge the gap between the white and black South Africans.

Mandela had to become incredibly patient and understanding to endure 27 years in prison. He kept his eyes fixed on the most significant benefit of the South African nation; liberation of the oppressed. The identity he built united the country.

Understand, our minds and bodies have an inseparable connection. We harness mirror neurons to model others and sharpen our skills with people, as well as our ability to reason. Yes, Mandela successfully navigated with social intelligence, but there was also an element of intuition. He placed himself into the mind of his oppressors, instead of fueling negativity with more negativity.

Each world-class example we've discussed had to refine their social intelligence. Building an identity, without understanding how to interact with people, will diminish your creativity and success. Challenges will arise as you interact with others; they include judging, politics, and criticism. Let's discuss the master steps to rise above these problems.

Nikola Tesla

Nikola Tesla died a poor man, despite significant contributions to society in wireless communication, AC motors, artificial intelligence, and smartphones. One of Tesla's most substantial weaknesses was his social intelligence. Tesla's possessed creative brilliance, but his business acumen was lacking. As a result, notable inventors: Thomas Edison and George Westinghouse gained financial success from his work.

Tesla became obsessed with transmitting energy wireless in the early 1900s. He planned to craft a system where people could communicate wirelessly. Consider this; Tesla was so far ahead that he was trying to create cell phone towers at the start of the 20th century. Its name was the "Free Energy Project," and the funding came from investors such as J.P. Morgan.

In 1901, Tesla conducted work on the project at a site on Long Island, New York, called Wardenclyffe. The location included a lab, transmission tower, and power plant. However, Tesla started losing funding as his investors lost faith. Ultimately, by 1915, the Free Energy Project failed. The location fell into foreclosure and was sold for scraps to pay off debts. But, Tesla's rival Guglielmo Marconi pushed forward in his work on radio technology, with backing from Thomas Edison and Andrew Carnegie.

Despite patenting over 300 inventions in his lifetime, Tesla lacked the social intelligence needed for success. Tesla was highly introverted, even reclusive, and demonstrated strange behavior. He completely missed the importance of communication with his investors. Still, no matter how brilliant he was, he needed other people to help him achieve his highest purpose.

Besides funding issues, Tesla became engrossed in a war with Edison over whose electrical current would power the Earth. Despite Alternating Current (AC) -Tesla's current- being superior to Direct Current (DC) - Edison's current- Thomas Edison gained favor. Edison won because of social intelligence; he marketed it far better than Tesla.

Remember this: **Let your work communicate, but never ignore the importance of other people in achieving your goals.** Make your work easily understood by others, care for people, and demonstrate your work's positive effects on humanity.

Also, prepare to accept criticism. When you receive the input of others, you're showing your openness and willingness to work with groups. Always seek to produce the highest quality solutions because the results are what's real. Nobody argues with results because that's like arguing with weather, or gravity.

If you experience politics, and hidden agendas, keep in mind that your work will help shield you from the harmful intentions of others. Most importantly, don't consume yourself in senseless battles as Tesla did with Edison. Let your work speak for itself, stay mindful of the importance of social intelligence, and you'll navigate smoothly to your highest purpose while rising above others.

Choose Your Personality (Andy Warhol)

Second, it's vital to **choose your personality, consciously.** Andy Warhol displayed a talent for drawing and painting in his early teens. His career began doing illustrations for companies such as Harper's Bazaar and Vogue. However, it wasn't long before Warhol designed a new personality for himself.

Warhol was best known for his mass-productions of paintings that depicted everyday objects; One of his most famous is the Campbell Soup can. In 1962, Warhol opened an art studio, designed to produce these items in quantity. He called it "The Factory," and he hired art workers to mass-produce his art.

Warhol was considered a pop icon with a unique personality. For starters, he began replacing his hair with blond and silver wigs. He loved cats and produced many pieces with them, and he produced over 300 strange experimental underground films. Some described his personality as Dr. Jekyll and Mr. Hyde. He urinated on some paintings because he believed it creates unique colors, and he was a devout Catholic.

Nicknamed "Drella" (a mix between Dracula and Cinderella), Warhol was notoriously tricky to figure out when interviewed. Instead of allowing people to assign labels to him, Warhol crafted the personality he wanted the world to see. Unless you create your character, as Warhol did, others can assign you personality traits based on who they perceive you to be.

Your focus can get lost in a sea of drama as people's judgments devour your attention. This distraction only serves to take you further away from accomplishing your highest purpose. So, choose who you want to become, so you control how others view you. Remember, you can recreate yourself an infinite number of times to suit your needs.

Like Warhol, never stay the same, and keep ahead of people by assuming new characters. It's vital to craft your personality, so you can effectively navigate the different personality types you will encounter on your way to success. This shift in figures isn't wrong or malicious; quite the opposite, by shifting yourself, you're expressing concern for others by communicating in a style that more closely matches theirs.

If you were direct and assertive, and you needed help from someone who's docile, approaching them very directly is a sure way not to get what you want. However, if you matched their style, you'd make them feel comfortable, validated, and appreciated. People help those they like and who they think are just like them. Craft your characters, and you will become more influential.

People Do The Craziest Things (Randy Moss)

Next, understand that **we can't escape the ridiculous behavior of some people.** There are simply a lot of people that have a different set of objectives in life. Often, those objectives get them in trouble. Whether these people are looking for instant gratification, attention, vanity, or drama, they make other people's lives difficult.

Former NFL player, Randy Moss, has been described as one of the most arrogant players in history. Moss had a temper that flared up whenever his team was losing. Also, outside of the football field, his decisions got him into trouble regularly.

In 2000, Moss paid $25,000 in fines for deciding to squirt an NFL referee with water. Later that year, he spent another $25,000 in penalties for laying hands on a ref. Just one year after, in 2001, Moss paid $15,000 in fines and was forced to attend anger management over verbal abuse after losing a game.

$1200 and 40 hours of community service later, Moss completed his sentence in 2002 for bumping a traffic cop with his car; there was marijuana in the vehicle during the incident. Then, September and November of 2003, Moss paid $10,000 in total fines for a fight and unsportsmanlike conduct.

Despite his talent, Moss is an example of someone who makes people's lives more difficult. He ignored the long-term problems his decisions were creating, yet regularly embroiled himself in short-term drama; this behavior suggests a lack of common sense.

The difficulty is that our emotions are contagious. It's difficult not to be affected when we're around people who act ridiculous. It's challenging because these people are annoying, irritating, and continually searching for trouble. Your tendency to stoop to their level makes you feel confused as you lose your focus.

Don't try to change or persuade these people; it's a waste of time and effort that needs to be devoted to your purpose. Remember: those types of people exist, they're just a part of life. Keep in mind, we all have moments where we make poor decisions; we lose control of ourselves. We're emotional creatures, and it's part of who we are.

The difference is, you can choose to be conscious of your behavior, and choose to accept these people for who they are, instead of trying to get them to act differently. It's nearly inevitable that you'll deal with these people. Consciously focus on where you're going, and what's vital, while ignoring the "noise."

Answer this, how can you turn their poor behavior into your benefit? Or, how can you turn their foolishness into lessons of what not to do? By choosing to see their actions in this context, you're transforming their mistakes into your advantages.

If you don't feel cut out to deal with the politics and maneuvering required of networking with people, then avoid it as often as possible. Alternatively, you can delegate social responsibilities to someone with the strength to effectively network. This delicate side of humanity presents itself in larger groups, so whatever your purpose is, you can minimize politics by choosing to start smaller. Remember, fewer people means fewer politics.

Lastly, learn and practice the basics of human interactions so you can recognize people with hidden agendas and win over tough people. As the story of Tesla demonstrated, you can't completely cut yourself off from others. By cutting ourselves off from others, we degrade our ability to learn, grow, and master our purpose.

Andy Warhol's Guidance

"When people are ready to, they change. They never do it before then, and sometimes they die before they get around to it. You can't make them change if they don't want to, just like when they do want to, you can't stop them."
— Andy Warhol

Chapter 5: Expand Your Knowledge & Creativity

As your skills and knowledge grow, so too must your boldness. Our brains continuously want to expand and take action. The most significant barrier to your success is your mindset. The people that are the most reserved are insecure with sharing their knowledge. They're scared of opening themselves to feedback from others, even if they have a deeper understanding of the topic. What inevitably occurs is that these people blend in with the group, and play by the rules of others.

Instead of being reserved, actively seek knowledge, and enhance your skills. Different fields of expertise will expand your mind and create new associations that were not present. Challenges get resolved by approaching from different angles, and it's your open mind that will empower you to craft solutions when others are closed off.

By thinking in dimensions, you bring yourself closer to the reality of situations. When you move closer to reality, you always move closer to the truth. With your fluid mind, you will be willing to reshape your beliefs to suit you. The closer you get to the facts of life, the more you'll be rewarded for following the laws of nature.

Moving Closer To Reality (Ray Dalio)

Ray Dalio, the billionaire hedge fund investor, wrote in his book *Principles* that it's vital to embrace reality and deal with it effectively. Working with reality means embracing radical truth and radical transparency in everything we do. Being radically truthful and transparent is uncomfortable to start because we don't tend to be completely open and honest.

Many people don't want to hurt other's feelings, or they don't want to make themselves feel vulnerable. Adopting these two principles gives our work and relationships more meaning. As Dalio suggests, the laws of reality didn't come from people; they're gifted to us by nature. Since nature has used its system to evolve for millions of years, we can use it to grow ourselves.

Take our brains; for example, we have evolved the ability to self-reflect. We're the only species that can do this; other species operate on instincts alone. The lion doesn't imagine itself as its prey, and the gazelle doesn't put itself in the mind of its predator.

Have you ever reflected on how closely we interact with these laws? Without discovering the laws of gravity, we could not fly a plane. To master land, sea, and air, we have invented numerous solutions that came from modeling animals; nature did not copy our inventions. Dalio's success has come from thinking in dimensions, studying different (seemingly unrelated) fields to expand his knowledge, and create new distinctions in his mind.

To think about your purpose dimensionally, you need to have a profound knowledge of the subject, and you need to be open to absorb different sectors of information. Some examples include studying money and psychology, or nature and business. However, to master these associations, we need to be actively involved in our mentorship and conquer the fundamentals of the purpose we choose.

When you can execute on the fundamentals without thinking, you'll be ready to expand your knowledge into different subjects. Understand: what we learn from our mentors can also make our minds rigid if we lose focus. When we stop adapting and changing, we freeze ourselves in a single way of thinking, closing our brain to other possibilities.

Keeping your mind fluid means always keeping it out of its comfort zone, never holding on to thoughts or emotions that don't serve you. Like a child, your mind needs to stay active, curious, and filled with wonder.

Expanding your knowledge will occur, first, by deciding your highest purpose. This mission needs to align with who you are; keep your mind fluid, be ready to soak up knowledge, and prepare your mental state for achievement.

Stay on guard against the human emotions that ruin success. By avoiding emotional traps, aligning with nature's laws to make decisions in reality, and keeping your mind open, you cannot fail. We need to begin expanding your knowledge with our first step, deciding your highest purpose.

The purpose you choose in your life is uniquely suited to who you are. It involves everything you are—personality, mind, spirit, body, and emotions. For instance, this book didn't get written without considerable research, experience, time, and effort. Throughout its writing, there have been challenges, and triumphs that you don't see.

Nonetheless, through determination, focus, grit, faith, and grace, you're reading these pages. The takeaway is that what you decide to devote yourself to matters. Even the most incredible figures in history would have been colossal failures if they didn't choose their purpose based on their inclinations. They would have lost interest, and wouldn't have the total commitment required for excellence.

Here's a clue, what do you obsess over? Think about what causes you to get up earlier than usual, forget to eat, stay up late, and forget everything around you. What have you gotten so intensely focused on that time is a blur? Every historical example in this book shares a quality; they were obsessed with something.

Your obsession will push you past all failures where others would have quit. Those days of tedious work, with no reward in sight, will be manageable because of your compulsion to continue. People who criticize you will not stop you from continuing because your mission is too compelling. Remember: where focus flows, the energy goes.

Dalio focuses his energy on seeing life as a game, with puzzles to solve. He says that by figuring them out, his reward is "gems" (principles) that help him improve his ability to make effective decisions. As he collects more gems, the game gets harder, and he ascends to new levels.

This game has plenty of emotions that can elevate us or bring us down. However, Dalio says it's when his emotions and logic align that he makes the best decisions. One of your most significant feelings is the feeling of *commitment* to the purpose you choose. Trying to reach success with anything less than total commitment always creates poor outcomes.

Also, being motivated by money is temporary and will not create total commitment. People will feel the lack of substance in your final product and respond accordingly. However, your dedication, commitment, and obsession will speak through your work. Nothing feels more authentic than something created with love and devotion.

You cannot make this choice based on intellect, and your intelligence will not push you above the need for having a passion for your purpose. As Dalio said, Dreams + Reality + Determination = A Successful Life. Imagine a horizontal line: on the left side is your desire to savor life, and on the right side is your desire to make an impact. Where do you fall on this continuum? Are you obsessed with savoring your life, making an impact, or both?

Whatever purpose you decide will be close to reality, and align with your natural strengths. Just by following these criteria, you will move on a unique path. You're on the right track are when people resist you, make fun of you, or don't support your decision. Also, your purpose should be a bit of a stretch for your current abilities; you should need to grow into it. Your obsessed nature will find you the energy and drive to match your ambition.

Next, you must never make decisions according to your pay. Pursuing your purpose does not guarantee financial security or feelings of comfort. As you continue on your path, you won't always be sure if you'll see a return on your work. Human beings crave a sense of control, of safety; they like knowing when things will occur.

Not knowing if or when payment is coming causes discomfort and anxiety. The feeling is too unstructured for many, too loose. We also care what others think of us and how we present ourselves to our peers. With a focus on pleasing others, it's difficult to create anything of value because we adopt the typical behavior of the people closest to us.

If you base your decisions on your financial and emotional safety, you'll never create the pressure you need to produce your best work. Imagine a deserted island with no one to rescue you. You'll need to explore the island, do whatever it takes to thrive, and use whatever you have, get in the water, and create results.

Now that you understand the importance of thinking in different dimensions, we need to discuss how. Our behaviors can harden our minds as time passes. Think about what you do the same way every day. Routines create a sense of order in our lives, we prefer to know what to expect, and we like what we know.

Honestly, routines keep us from wasting time; humans love habits. Nonetheless, when we are learning anything new, our minds work harder because we're not good at it yet. With time, we increase our skill level, but we also get stuck in ways of thinking and acting. If we're not careful, we close off the ideas of others and resist change.

Nobody is immune to this effect, so you need tactics to expand the mind and be receptive to other people's ideas. Think of your brain as being a hard mass of dried playdoh. We're going to stretch it in different directions, loosen it up, and prepare it to incorporate new colors (different thoughts).

The Idea Meritocracy (Ray Dalio)

The first tactic is an idea meritocracy. Loosening our minds requires us to stop judging everything around us. The very idea behind an idea meritocracy is that it doesn't matter *who* is right; it but *what* is right. It's critical to entertain the perspectives of other people, experiencing their emotions about the subject.

By not forming a judgment about them or their ideas, you're pulling your mind in a different dimension, opening it for reshaping. Idea meritocracies place the weight on who is the most believable. So, instead of thinking we know best, it's encouraging open disagreement to arrive at the most effective solutions.

Surround yourself with others willing to disagree with you, open to productive discussions, new ideas, and expanding their minds. If you haven't met those people yet, read books, and listen to podcasts that are polar opposite to your beliefs. View yourself as though you're never the smartest person in the room and always ready to learn from others. Consider that life is ever-changing, and we can't effectively grasp what is real.

Also, with an idea meritocracy based on how believable people are, and an environment that rewards productive discussion, you give yourself the highest chance of making decisions that align with reality.

Ray Dalio's company is called Bridgewater Associates, and they are one of the original adopters of an idea meritocratic culture. As Dalio says, "A pervasive Idea Meritocracy = Radical Truth + Radical Transparency + Believability-Weighted Decision Making." Understand: this idea may seem fresh now, or it may seem stale and old. Either way, likely, this idea will someday go away as we evolve.

Just as we find humor in the things that generations before us believed and did. It's likely that someday our ideas will seem outdated also. So, don't fall in love with your belief system, and never fall into a permanent mindset. Use this idea meritocracy to open your mind, and use the most credible information to shape your decisions.

Ray Dalio's Guidance

"Embrace tough love. In my own life, what I want to give to people, most importantly, to people I love, is the power to deal with reality to get what they want." – Ray Dalio

---

Release (Steve Jobs)

The second tactic is to *release*. Our minds think in associations. Whenever something enters our minds, it's compared with our beliefs. Our brains are always seeking to answer three questions: How are things alike? How are things different? And how do items interact with each other? The best way to help your mind answer these questions is to stop focusing on answering the questions; to release your focus.

When we immerse ourselves in an activity, our attention becomes finely concentrated. Imagine your focus as a light: It can be a laser pointer or broad like a flashlight. The more singular our focus is, the more we shut off everything around us. You wouldn't try to light a dark room with a laser pointer, would you?

If that dark room had opportunities all around it, we would miss them because of our "laser pointer." By using the "flashlight" and broadening the light in the room, you're opening yourself to see opportunities. To help our mind unleash its flashlight, we need to release our focus and relax into a peaceful state. When we are at ease, our brains expand and absorb more.

The late Steve Jobs was well-known for doing his creative thinking while walking. He would also hold important meetings during walks, instead of sitting in meeting rooms. By letting your brain process under states of relaxation, you're inviting unexpected breakthroughs to occur. Walking, dreaming, and meditation are all crucial strategies for releasing your mind and attracting solutions.

To start, go wide in your research. You'll create connections by combining fields of study. For any beliefs you hold, find people and criteria that try to disprove you. Trust that you will feel stimulation from the different dimensions of what you learn. With this mind-stretching, you'll create the environment you need for breakthrough thoughts.

To assist your research, journal after naps, walks, and meditation. Have your journal available to write down every moment of inspiration that strikes you. Be as detailed as possible in your journaling, and document images, phrases, dialogues, and everything that happens when your subconscious mind takes over.

Think of this as piecing together various unrelated ideas into a working concept. The goal of these actions is to connect different topics into a design with a potent creative force. Then, take action and try the ideas that come to you.

Our minds generally think in terms of pictures, not words. We are storytellers, which is why we use metaphors to explain ideas. Comparing your *focus* to a flashlight or a laser pointer, in the earlier example, instantly directed your mind's imagination. Thinking in pictures can make sense, for instance, comparing apples to oranges. Or it can be creative, such as imagining the world as a big machine. Regardless, think of ways you can use pictures to loosen your mind and establish new neural connections.

Steve Jobs Guidance

"Creativity is just connecting things."
— Steve Jobs

Harness Your Consciousness (The Wright Brothers)

The third tactic is to harness your consciousness. In 1878, Wilbur and Orville Wright received a toy helicopter as a gift from their father. Their father, Milton, traveled to preach and was away from home often. The toy thrilled both Wright brothers, who developed a deep passion for flight.

At the start of the 20th century, Orville and Wilbur Wright transitioned from bikes to airplanes. There was a heated competition to be the first to develop a flying machine that worked, and the Wright brothers kept tabs on the latest research of aviator Otto Lilienthal. That is until a crash took Lilienthal's life.

This event was the catalyst that motivated Orville and Wilbur to enter the race and test their ideas. Kitty Hawk, North Carolina, was well known for wind, so the Wright brothers set up their operations there. Interestingly, the Wright brothers were the underdogs compared to other researchers who had large pools of funding.

Still, what the Wright brothers possessed was a fresh perspective. It was their *consciousness* that enabled them to see the creative details that others missed. To design the wings of their flying machine, they considered how birds already fly, modeling their design according to nature. They crafted them at an angle, just like a bird's wings, in a process known as "wing warping." December 17, 1903, is the first day that a controlled flight succeeded.

The Wright Brothers' astounding feat happened because the brothers suspected that nature could show them how to fly, instead of trying to create a new process like their competitors. Then, they tested what they suspected, moving closer to the reality of flight. What we *think* and what is *real* regularly interact with each other.

The Wright Brothers competitors *thought* they would use what they know to invent the flying machine.

They didn't test their thoughts against reality to let nature reveal the truth. By aligning with natural laws, Orville and Wilbur Wright's discovery transcended the limited capabilities of people.

Nonetheless, it all begins with being conscious of our surroundings. Remember, our minds are an evolutionary gift from the earliest days of the human race. Parts of our brain, such as the amygdala, are ancient. Survival depended on our ancestors being conscious of their surroundings and imagining what things meant, thinking in pictures. Through imagination, our ancestors could figure out the hidden truths of the world around them.

Today, we see people jump to assumptions about what something means, without considering if it's true. Some speak as if things are a fact, just based on their experience. These people don't profoundly observe or consider alternative possibilities. Letting their minds run wild, they decide what reality is, and push it on others, without discovering if it's true.

Alternatively, some researchers have all of the data they need. But unlike the Wright Brothers, they never use it to take action. These people are too afraid to pose a question because they believe speculation has no place in research. However, if it weren't for Orville and Wilbur *suspecting* that birds are the key to flight, history wouldn't be the same.

Be curious, conscious, and form questions about what you see. Don't only see your surroundings, but develop theories and try to prove them with data. By approaching life with such an analytic and artistic method, your answers are more likely to be close to reality.

Let's apply this to your purpose. For instance, imagine you intend to make an impact on others. You can either create a product or provide a service to the public. However, you might see that they're not as enthusiastic (initially) about your purpose as you are. It's because what you *think* people want is different than the *reality* of what they want. It's better to test what you believe people desire and improve on it with iterations.

Instead of guessing, people's feedback and iterations will improve what you provide because you'll come closer to reality. As you move closer to what is real, you will see more demand for what you have. People who have tremendous success have it because they provided solutions that align closely with reality.

Wilbur Wright's Guidance

"The desire to fly is an idea handed down to us by our ancestors who...looked enviously on the birds soaring freely through space...on the infinite highway of the air." – Wilbur Wright

---

Identify And Break Your Habits (Steve Jobs)

The fourth tactic is to use your conscious mind to identify and break your habits. We have thousands of shortcuts we use every day to save time and mental effort. We open a door by accessing our past thoughts and experiences to generalize how the door handle functions. Can you imagine if you could only open a door by analyzing a memory of you using that exact door handle in the past?

While these shortcuts help us, we also hurt our progress by applying them to a lot of other parts of our life. As an example, we place people into different "buckets" based on our past experiences, instead of taking the time to find out who they are and think through various possibilities. This behavior is our way of being, a collection of habits. To stretch your mind and change these habits, we'll go over the general shortcuts we use and strategies to deal with them effectively.

We already touched on generalizing and making assumptions. This behavior is the first habit we need to work out. Most of our opinions are rooted in very few facts. Our views align with what we have experienced in the past, and it's easy for us to put our general assumptions onto others. "If it happened to *me* that way, it will happen to *you* the same way."

This habit stems from a lazy approach to understanding our surroundings. There's a lack of attention to detail and no thorough analysis. Even worse, we take these shortcut assumptions and develop firm beliefs around them.

Because this pattern stems from casting a "wide net," the solution is to narrow your scope to the smaller details; instead of looking at the forest, look at the trees. Instead of generalizing, Steve Jobs took a calligraphy class at Reed College; he considered it an essential course. Because of that class, he obsessed over the tiniest details in computer fonts. When Steve proposed the idea that people can change fonts on a computer, it was a revolutionary idea for the time.

Still, because of Jobs's attention to *small* details, he accomplished his *broad* vision of every computer having font choices. Make decisions based on the little details, form questions around what you notice with your consciousness; see how individual pieces come together to form the whole. Focusing on the small bits of information will take your mind away from placing things in general categories and bring you towards the truth of any event. But, never forget that the smallest details make up the more broad machine. Jobs obsessed over fonts but knew that they benefited the whole computer.

Identifying Problems But Not Causes

The next shortcut we use is to identify problems, without getting to their root cause. Imagine an unsupervised child drawing all over your walls with crayons. Many people shortcut to what happened (the child drawing on the walls), but never ask themselves how it occurred (the child was left unsupervised with their crayons). Can you see the difference?

To overcome this habit, observe the details that lead up to the undesired effect, the pieces that make up the whole machine. Yes, the child was left unsupervised with crayons, but ask, why do you have to supervise the child? Why aren't they associating that coloring belongs on paper? Always look to yourself as being part of the problem, and solution.

Reflecting this way, we have to look at the little details that create our consequences. By improving our ability to connect the dots, we enhance our ability to think and make better decisions. Look at nature; for instance, everything affects everything else. Everything has a relationship, an association that makes up the circle of life. Think in these terms, identify the pieces, and you can determine how the whole picture. You can choose at any time to change your thinking in this way, and start understanding how things work.

Considering The Visible And Not The Invisible (Tesla Motors)

Our second mental shortcut is considering the visual, without considering the invisible. Imagine your mind's eye as having a lens with two settings. You can turn it to visualize what you can see, or you can change the setting to see the invisible.

Take your work, for example, is your company focused on cost-efficiency, or doing things better? Or are they focused on what the customers are not getting? The former is the first lens and is the most common. The latter requires effort, creativity, and is more complicated. However, the latter also has far more potential because it steers the company by what its customers demand.

Considering the invisible is an exercise in creativity because we're expanding our thinking past its usual limited range while opening our minds to new possibilities. Look at Tesla Motors, founded in 2003, after General motors stopped its prototype production of an electric vehicle (EV-1). Tesla's mission has always been to mass-produce high-quality electric cars.

Most cars in 2003-2004 were still running on gasoline, but the founders of Tesla Motors shifted their lens and saw what customers didn't have. The electric car market wasn't fully visible in 2003, it was there, but there was potential because the demand for the cars wasn't too apparent.

Understand that our emotional state colors these lenses. We will see our surroundings differently based on how we feel at any given moment. For instance, if we feel confident, we'll notice more opportunities, but we might downplay the risks involved. What this means is that whenever you shift your lens, change your emotional state as well.

Take the pain of growth, for example; Ray Dalio says that Pain + Reflection = Progression. He suggests that pain is nature's way of showing us that we're moving in the right direction. You, too, must change how you define your emotions, it will change what you see through your lens, and will help you make decisions that get you positive results.

Finally, always look at the second and third-order effects of your decisions, and Imagine the opposite result. For example, exercise can be painful, but that pain is only the first-order result. The discomfort of working out leads to the second-order consequence of excellent health. Now, what is the opposite result? Not working out isn't painful, but can lead to the second-order effect of health problems. Take invisible challenges that could occur and decide how you can turn them into advantages.

Elon Musk's Guidance

"When Henry Ford made cheap, reliable cars, people said, 'Nah, what's wrong with a horse?' That was a huge bet he made, and it

worked." – Elon Musk, CEO of Tesla

Confirmation Bias

The last mental shortcut we rely on is confirmation bias. Humans need to have explanations for everything because it gives us a sense of control in the world. Still, when we adopt beliefs, we can lose our objectivity and only search for answers that make our belief right. With our mindset closed, we're unwilling to take in new information that can tarnish our cherished thoughts.

Understand, there's much personal growth in the thoughts that don't fit our beliefs. Fill yourself with curiosity and investigate the ideas and patterns that closed-minded people ignore. By doing this, you expose your views to being wrong and stretch your mind to absorb new dimensions of thought.

As COVID-19 presses forward, there have been businesses that are winning, losing, and discovering new opportunities. In April 2020, dairy farmers dumped thousands of gallons of milk because they claimed there are no buyers. The dairy farmers are stuck in their ways of thinking before the virus. Nonetheless, do you know how many different products come from the milk they're dumping?

Spoiled milk creates everything from baked goods to salad dressing. Imagine you are an entrepreneur that approaches the dairy farmers and buys up their spoiled milk for next to nothing. You can repurpose it into a product such as a creamy salad dressing because you know people are stuck at home having more family dinners.

The dairy farmers don't repurpose their milk because they view themselves as just dairy farmers and nothing more. But this is their incredible opportunity to use what they have to grow. Can you see how we can improve by challenging our original beliefs? Working these different angles is how we innovate, progress, and ensure we get to the future before others.

Learning From Our Ancestors

Before the invention of language, our ancient ancestors needed to rely on alternate forms of communication. Thinking in terms of pictures, and using their senses, our ancestors evolved their minds to notice trends in their environment. They learned to navigate using the sun and stars, became adept at building tools, and developed excellent hand-eye coordination.

With language, we gained the ability to think in words as well as pictures. The advantage of this invention is that we learned to communicate the images in our minds. Thinking in these terms gave us layers of thought and mental agility. However, over time we became too dependent on language, which diminished our senses.

Our heavy reliance on verbal communication has made sensory acuity less critical. We no longer rely as heavily on our ability to think by touching, seeing, and smelling our environment. Reaching your purpose means imagining what isn't real yet. As vital as language is, you need to create ways to involve your senses.

If your highest purpose were to serve others as a chef, you wouldn't just communicate your dream. You would imagine yourself in the kitchen, feeling the heat from the stove. You would smell the food as it cooks, observe your work coming together to form the final dish, and touch the ingredients with your fingers.

Using your senses and thinking in multiple layers (pictures and words) is the most powerful way to use your brain. You can see how limited language is when you experience something so moving that it doesn't have a word to describe it. Words have their limits, and relying too heavily on language restrains us from our full capabilities.

Consider this, how easy is it to remember an image? Let's say, a picture of your bedroom? Pretty simple. Instead, What if I asked you to remember only ten different words, it wouldn't be as simple. For most, our conscious memory has limitations. However, an image contains many items that we simultaneously remember. Thinking in terms of pictures is a shortcut; it's pre-verbal, and words are simply our way of sharing these pictures so that others can form their image.

Practice this by creating ways to transmute words into pictures, use metaphors and analogies to conjure images that you can draw on. Then, make real illustrations; create visual models, diagrams, and charts. Seeing information in a different form will cause you to think differently about it.

Alessandro Volta was an Italian physicist that invented the first electric battery, providing a source of constant current. The electricity that we take for granted today was non-existent in Volta's time. Remember, Volta had to think in pictures because an electrical current wasn't visible. By visualizing that electrical currents must flow between two metals, Volta tested his theory by using his tongue to check the flow of electricity.

The physical expression of Volta's imagination of electrical current was the voltaic pile. It used the combination of silver and zinc, or copper and pewter soaked with paper and saltwater to generate an electrical current.

Volta was thinking with his body, not just his mind. The prevailing thought at the time was that living tissue conducted electrical currents, then known as "animal electricity." However, Volta kept his mind loose and open to different possibilities; he didn't just approach electrical current with intellect. He tested the relationship between two metals without living tissue and illustrated his concept for the voltaic pile.

Alessandro Volta's Guidance

"You must be ready to give up even the most attractive ideas when experiment shows them to be wrong." – Alessandro Volta

---

The Importance Of Pressure And Reflection

When we work towards any purpose, our initial experience is one of excitement and enthusiasm. Our mission aligns with who we are, and we become emotionally attached. We start to imagine the outcomes we desire and create specific images in our minds. You'll know you're in this phase when you feel that what you're producing is inadequate compared to your expectation.

As you progress, you'll uncover mistakes that you didn't see when you started. As challenges arise, your purpose can feel flat as the initial enthusiasm wears off; you may wonder if you're even doing something you love. At this point, many give up and try something different, but some push ahead and give it more effort. But this can backfire because it creates more pressure.

An activity that was once new, vibrant, and teeming with possibilities now seems mundane. If you want to surpass this phase, it's essential to realize that the only way is to keep pushing ahead. But the pressure you feel is part of the process and serves the function of alerting you to step away and reflect. Take a walk, take a nap, or do another activity; just take your mind's focus off of your purpose.

After a decade of trying to connect chemical elements, On February 17th, 1869, Dimitry Mendeleev fell into a deep sleep from exhaustion. As he dreamt, he reported visualizing the Periodic Table of Elements falling into place. They danced into their order according to the sounds of the chamber music playing in the adjacent room.

As the dream continued, the elements fell into place according to their atomic weight, from lightest to the heaviest. After everything was in place, Mendeleev woke up with the foundation for a near-perfect Periodic Table of Elements.

Mendeleev made a tremendous scientific breakthrough by letting go of his pressure to find the answer. He removed himself from the problem by sleeping and reflected on the response he received from his subconscious.

Mendeleev realized that he had hit his point of maximum pressure. He was single-minded in solving the mystery of the Periodic Table of Elements, but he was stuck. Upon reaching this point, our minds are telling us to stop. Through sheer exhaustion, Mendeleev got his answer from a decade's worth of connections that had formed in his subconscious mind.

In his dream state, he was relieved of pressure, where his mind was able to loosen and find the answer from a different angle. His subconscious mind took over and provided the solution that had been incubating below the surface.

To tap into this state, you need to build pressure. Build as much as possible, and then release it by stepping away from your activity. Take your mind off of your purpose and only reflect once the answer presents itself to you.

In 1970, Apollo 13 was flying to the moon when an explosion happened inside the ship. It damaged the air filtration system that was keeping the astronauts alive. If mission control in Houston didn't develop a solution, in a matter of hours, the crew would be dead from lethal levels of carbon dioxide.

The scene was all hands on deck as scientists, technicians, and engineers worked at a feverish pace to solve the problem. Mission control created mockups of air filters by only using items that were present on Apollo 13. With almost no time left, the team invented an ugly solution, so simple that they coached the astronauts through building it. The filter they created saved three people that day.

The takeaway from this story is how vital it is for us to have pressure in our lives. When we feel as though there are no time limits to our work, our minds ease up. This state of relaxation makes it more difficult for us to utilize our minds entirely because our thoughts aren't associating. To overcome this relaxation, and think at a higher level, create time pressure for yourself.

For example, if you have three months to complete something, give yourself a week instead. Adding this pressure will force you to elevate yourself to meet the challenge, just as mission control rose to save three astronauts. Treat your life with a sense of urgency. Act as though you don't have all the time in the world, and notice how you'll start prioritizing and producing like never before.

Burn all the boats, back yourself into a corner, and force yourself to create a way out. You can create this tension by making yourself accountable to others. Tell people about your plans as though they've already happened, and make promises that you need to keep. These actions will spur your mind into a creative state where you'll rise to the occasion.

The Six Dangerous Feelings

No matter what our purpose is, we face certain feelings that can derail us if we don't deal with them first. These feelings are different than mental challenges, and handling them will ensure that you never lose valuable time and clarity.

The first dangerous feeling is restlessness. Whether from boredom or anxiety, restless people tend to be impatient. You stop short of completing work, or you look for shortcuts to get around the hard work required. When people are restless, the feeling is clouding sound judgment. You're motivated by the things that come quick, instead of the things that will last. However, the most meaningful and lasting things take patience.

When we're restless, we value what's familiar. We do things the same way because we know what to expect. Acting in this way, we lose the drive we once had for our purpose. What once inspired you, now feels unfulfilling, and it shows in the results.

Warren Buffett has a few simple secrets to his wealth. However, they're not simple to many. One of his principles is the importance of patience and discipline. Buffett is always thinking about the future, not the past.

His strategy for investing (and life) is to buy and hold. He's lived in the same state his whole life; he lives in the same home purchased in the late 1950s and drives one car that he tends to keep for many years.

Buffett calls his investing strategy, "buy and hold *and hold*." He's known to tell his shareholders that his favorite holding period for stocks is forever. Instead of being restless and looking for instant gratification, Buffett lets his success slowly accumulate over a lifetime. However, this behavior is challenging for many, so the best solution is to develop a love for stress.

For example, people in the gym put their bodies through equivalent physical stress because they understand the lifetime benefits on their health. Like Buffett, you must practice patience, and find enjoyment in overcoming your restlessness. Practice pushing your limits, while repelling the easy path.

The next dangerous feeling is fear. As we develop our system and improve our skills within our purpose, we start to see success. The danger in this progress is that it can lock us into our habits, making us afraid to change what's working. Why try something else when **X** gets me **Y**? Fear of failing restricts your ability to be creative and evolve beyond your current skills.

When you began learning your purpose, you had to resist fear and be assertive in your approach. That assertiveness is still required when you reach higher levels of success. To innovate, we need to be willing to challenge the rules, even the ones we created for ourselves. With the rapid expansion of technology, humanity has never needed innovation more than they do now.

However, letting fear determine your comfort zone will create poor results, and the world will pass you. We see this behavior in people who want to keep all of their processes and procedures the same. One change to the company's systems and these people are outraged. You'll triumph over this feeling, as soon as you open your mind, and make innovation your priority, instead of security.

The third dangerous feeling is arrogance. If we don't express discipline, our achievements can affect our ego. Failure delivers valuable lessons and insights that show us how to improve. Success, on the other hand, has far fewer lessons to teach. One of the worst events that can happen to people is when they succeed before an adequate number of failures.

Look at lottery winners, for instance, many gain tremendous wealth with no financial foundation. They never went through the *struggle* to build massive wealth, so they don't know how to control it; many end up bankrupt a few years after winning.

When others begin celebrating you for your accomplishments within your purpose, it can cloud your vision. You may start to crave more praise, and you might convince yourself that you're brilliant, forgetting those that helped you along the way. Where you were once hungry to grow, now you crave attention. Understand: the ego will inevitably face a point where it meets reality once again, and when that happens, the consequences can be long-lasting.

Never forget that there is always someone in the world who is superior to us. Practice gratitude for your coaches and mentors, the giants whose shoulders you stood on. Lastly, find your inspiration in your life's work, your purpose, and fall in love with the journey. Success will inevitably draw people's attention, but you can use these practices to rise above the ego's desire for recognition.

The fourth dangerous feeling is pride. Watch how young kids see the world with amazement. The smallest objects strike them with feelings of fascination. As people mature, they take things for granted; everything stops being a mystery, we fall into our patterns, and life becomes all too familiar. We begin to believe "we already know" instead of approaching our lives with a sense of that childlike curiosity.

Set your pride aside and reconnect with the awe you possessed when you were little. Realize that you are one of almost 8 billion people on one of 100 billion planets. You are infinitely small, in a vast and evolving galaxy. Let this thought fill you with wonder because pride will only serve to diminish your connection with reality.

As we become more proficient with our purpose, our minds are teeming with unique ideas; we feel pride in our knowledge and what we have achieved. However, if we don't consciously practice gratitude, our ego can get in the way as we develop a sense of superiority. Pride narrows our minds, dulling our thoughts; our prior accomplishments don't matter because we stop growing in the present. Don't let feelings of pride get the best of you. Consciously maintain a child's spirit and always stay curious.

The fifth dangerous feeling is obstinance. You will always be learning your purpose; it's a lifelong pursuit. There will never come a time when you have finally "arrived" and know everything. Even when you have a firm grasp, your purpose will likely change, so you'll need to change.

Obstinance gets in the way because it's an unwillingness to change. We need to master our field of study but stay fluid so we can always challenge our beliefs; you must be willing to look at yourself with a critical eye. To avoid getting locked into any *way* of doing things, always search yourself, and question whether you're attached to an attitude or mindset.

    This habit isn't simple to adopt, especially when our cherished beliefs make us feel good. You might find yourself optimistic about something, which makes it difficult to be objective and consider its opposite. We crave positive emotions, not negative ones, and it's the act of challenging your positive emotions that takes an emotional toll.

    Still, this habit's objective is not to take away your fulfillment. The goal is to filter your beliefs so that you only possess ideas that are genuinely fulfilling. Looking beyond your optimism and considering other alternatives becomes more natural with practice. You'll overcome obstinance by feeling positivity and uncertainty simultaneously.

The sixth dangerous feeling is insecurity. When we're born, we go through a prolonged period where we depend on others. As you learn your purpose and practice under your teachers, you're reliant on them to provide you the right guidance to grow. However, a point always comes where we outgrow our teachers and need to take our independence.

You need to spread your wings, never rely on the opinions of your teachers or critics for validation. But, at the same time, never dismiss what others have to say about your work. Imagine you have two buckets, and separate criticism into the *constructive* bucket, and the *noise* bucket. Overcome insecurity and develop your voice by adopting the most vital lessons from your teachers, and dismissing what doesn't serve you. You'll never find how you want to express yourself if you allow feelings of insecurity from outside influences.

Create Yourself

We want to feel like we matter, we crave feelings of connection to people, and strive to find meaning in this world. Everywhere around us are distractions that seek to take us away from getting our needs met, and feeling fulfilled. Some include virtual reality, drugs, or dangerous sports. Just for a moment, it jolts us and makes us feel alive.

The vital distinction is to choose activities where we are *creating* instead of consuming. Have you noticed that consuming activities rarely bring us a sense of fulfillment? For example, eating, shopping, buying cars, or buying homes. Our satisfaction comes from what we create for others. If we consume education, it means little unless we use it to create value.

Creating can feel uncomfortable, but you must strive to be a creator, more than a consumer. The laws of nature always reward that which creates, and your reward will be the immense feeling of satisfaction you get from using your purpose to provide value for others. Happiness and fulfillment are always waiting and available to you as soon as you decide to create value for others.

Warren Buffett's Guidance

"Someone's sitting in the shade today because someone planted a tree a long time ago" – Warren Buffett

---

The school system doesn't teach us how to create ourselves and find our purpose. As we move through life, we learn much through experience and develop methods to get what we want. When we put additional positive pressure on ourselves, we evolve; think of steel forged in heat. Creativity is an absolute necessity when finding your purpose and working within it.

The stories to follow will contain strategies to unlock your imagination and expand your knowledge.

Expand Your Uniqueness (Ed Sheeran)

Before Ed ever became a grammy-winning singer/songwriter, he ran off to London, as a teenager, to hit the music scene. Sheeran started playing guitar from a very early age and writing music due to inspiration from musician, Damien Rice. At only 14 years old, Sheeran released an EP, *The Orange Room*, and quickly got to work, releasing back to back records in 2006 and 2007.

He was only getting started because by 2010, Ed was maneuvering his music through social media expertly, which lead to an opening act on tour, with an artist named Example. More importantly, the world started noticing him. Jamie Foxx took notice in 2010 and had Sheeran on Sirius XM, and by 2011 his EP hit second on Itunes (organically).

Sheeran signed with Atlantic records shortly after and released "+," which saw sales cross 1 million between the U.S. and United Kingdom. From there, he moved up to the next level, packing stadiums with Taylor Swift in support of her 2013 stadium tour: *The

Red Tour. 2014 was an excellent year for music when Ed released "X," which hit #1 and won him a grammy in 2016 for his hit song "Thinking Out Loud."

By 2017, he broke listening records on Spotify for his album, and hit #1 for his hit "Shape of You." Ed has made appearances in numerous movies and T.V. shows, can be found on Youtube playing in random public places, and never seems to be far from his guitar. He is a double threat that has proven time and again that he can write creative music, and perform.

From a young age, he knew music is his purpose. With little more than a backpack of clothes and his guitar, he set off to London to play. His uniqueness comes from the way he expresses himself through his music; he has never lost himself because he lets his actions speak through his art. Realize, Sheeran has built tremendous diversity and fluidity. His music doesn't rigidly adhere to a single style. From rap to rock, he expresses the flexibility of a man living his purpose.

Understand, in 2009 alone, Ed Sheeran, virtually unknown, played more than 300 live shows. Think of this time as Sheeran learning his purpose. After such a rigorous period, creativity flowed out from him as he released albums and EPs year after year. At that point, all of his learning and experience gave him unique ideas to combine different genres of music into creative works of art.

By continuing to express who he is, Sheeran touches people's emotions with his songs. His music has a different effect because you're listening to someone who doesn't play for money, but purpose and passion. When we live in this way and express ourselves despite fear, the money follows.

Notice that Ed Sheeran wasn't restless when he devoted a year to playing over 300 shows. Fear never got the best of him when he packed a backpack and moved to London as a teenager. Instead, he allowed his deepest desires to steer him. Trying to act in any other way comes across as inauthentic, and people can feel it.

Model Ed Sheeran and fall in love with your purpose for passion's sake, not profit, or vanity. Live authentically through your desire and let it be your voice. Anybody who devotes everything they are to their craft is bound to be authentic and express their personality.

Ed Sheeran's Guidance

"Do what you love, work as hard as you can, and make people happy." **– Ed Sheeran**

Our Hands Unlock Our Imagination (Steve Wozniak)

In 1976 Steve Wozniak (Woz) was an engineering intern at Hewlett-Packard when he designed a personal computer off of a new Intel 8080 microprocessor. Hewlett-Packard expressed no interest in his design, but Steve Jobs did. Apple was born from a belief in Steve Wozniak's invention, and out of Job's garage, the two began creating and selling circuit boards for the computer.

From 1976-1977 Wozniak built what would come to be known as the Apple II. It was compatible with a color monitor, included a power supply, and had a keyboard built into the design. The importance of the Apple II is that Wozniak created a smaller computer that appealed to more than tech hobby groups; he helped take personal computing mainstream.

Do you love your phone? Steve Wozniak's creation laid the foundation for the modern devices that we enjoy. Over time, Wozniak created upgrades for the

Apple II, such as floppy disk drives, and introduced a spreadsheet application called VisiCalc in 1979.

Besides the Apple II, Wozniak is well known for building a little creative device called the "Blue Box." Wozniak was at his house when he picked up a copy of Esquire Magazine that was lying around. Inside was an article written by Ron Rosenblum, titled "Secrets of the Blue Box-fiction." It was a story about a network of engineers that had special equipment with the capability to control the phone lines internationally.

Inspired by the story and its hero "Captain Crunch," Wozniak and Jobs paid a visit to the Stanford Linear Accelerator Center (SLAC) to search for a book with the frequencies of the phone networks. They found it.

Only a few weeks later, Wozniak's tinkering paid off. He created a digital blue box that could make phone calls internationally, for free, using a 2600 Hz frequency. (imagine a high E note or the sound of a toy whistle)

What's essential to grasp is that Steve Wozniak's creativity came from using his hands. The personal computer is arguably one of the most important creations of humanity. But, these machines were once very costly, took up entire rooms, and did much less than our portable devices today. Before the Apple II, the people interested in computers were niche groups of enthusiasts and programmers with deep technical experience.

And then there was Wozniak, who got his pleasure from getting into the nuts and bolts. His fulfillment came from working with his hands to create. It was the feeling of connecting with a project, and working it from start to finish (problems and all) that excited Wozniak and got his imagination flowing.

When we work with tools, we're connecting with our cerebral cortex. In today's society, there's more emphasis on reasoning than mechanical intelligence. Never forget that our brains developed over millions of years by what we built. Wozniak not only *created* things, but he *worked* with his inventions as well.

Through the process of *making* his inventions, he became deeply *connected* with his work. Wozniak solved problems in his designs because he could feel its issues. If you had an upset stomach, someone else doesn't feel it; only you do because you are one with your body. What Wozniak had was a vision of the Apple II as a whole, he could see the components necessary and eagerly worked to bring it together.

Jobs and Wozniak didn't have a ton of money. Still, they relied on imagination and used what they had to create a simple solution with mass appeal. If you want to expand your knowledge and ingenuity, get involved with an activity where you develop a deeper connection between your hands and eyes.

Steve Wozniak's Guidance

"If you are doing something for a grade or salary or a reward, it doesn't have as much meaning as creating something for yourself and your own life." – Steve Wozniak

Repurpose The Existing (Sara Blakely)

In March 2012, Sara Blakely became the youngest, self-created female billionaire in the world, according to Forbes Magazine. Her SPANX empire began with a pair of scissors and a problem to solve. Blakely had a party to attend and wanted to wear white pants. However, she couldn't find an undergarment that wouldn't show under the pants.

Blakely innovated by cutting the feet off of a pair of pantyhose and wearing them under the white pants. Since then, SPANX has grown to solve clothing issues with bras, leggings, activewear, underwear, and beyond by improving existing items.

Not only did she repurpose an existing item (undergarments), she used innovation to never invest in advertising. Instead, she traveled the country, modeling her product for large retail stores like Neiman Marcus. She also took second in Sir Richard Branson's reality show, *Rebel Billionaire*. Always marketing, Sara made countless appearances and reached a couple hundred million dollars in sales by 2010. By 2012, Blakely took partial ownership in the Atlanta Hawks and had full ownership of her billion-dollar company.

When we met at a growth conference in 2019, she said a vital creative practice is to take time to think about where your mind wanders because it's where your best thoughts arise. Whatever we want, we can write what we want to create, and our creative success comes from thinking through our challenge.

Take undergarments; for example, Blakely created a market because the industry stopped innovating. The undergarment industries got locked into activities that brought them success in the past. Still, their prior success didn't guarantee future results, and years passed as these companies did what they've always done.

SPANX rocked these companies because it was a billion-dollar solution hiding in plain sight. It brought an "edge" that didn't exist, rebelled against the old, and gave birth to the shapewear revolution.

Everywhere around us are old ideas that need repurposing. Because others get stuck in their conventions, you have a massive opportunity to innovate, just like Sara Blakely. SPANX started with a problem that needed solving. Start by reflecting on what you need to address. What do you want to create that suits your personality? Listen to that little voice inside.

Maybe you noticed a need that nobody is meeting, a service that you could do better yourself, a unique topic that needs a voice. Whatever it is, fill yourself with curiosity, and go against the grain of its current trend. Blakely didn't make SPANX out of focus groups or market research, but by creating what the current market was not providing her.

Take Blakely's example, look at the truth of what works, take the knowledge you've accumulated, and make room for yourself in the market by differentiating. We crave growth, progression, and relevant solutions that fit our generation. When you *Zag* instead of *Zig*, you'll capture an untapped market that was waiting for you.

Sara Blakely's Guidance

"Don't be intimidated by what you don't know. That can be your greatest strength and ensure that you do things differently from everyone else." – Sara Blakely

---

The Importance of Accidents (Sir Alexander Fleming)

Sir Alexander Fleming was born on Lochfield farm, in East Ayrshire, Scotland, on August 6, 1881. Alexander had four full siblings; as well as four half-siblings from his father's first marriage. Before moving with his brother (Thomas) in London, in 1895, Alexander went to the Louden Moor Elementary School, then attended Darvel, and finally, the Kilmarnock Academy in 1894. However, Fleming finished his primary schooling at London's Regent Street Polytechnic.

In 1900, Fleming joined the Territorial Army, serving until 1914 in the London Scottish Regiment. During his service, he started studying the medical field in 1901 at the University of Londons' St. Mary's Hospital Medical School. Just seven years later, he was acknowledged as the top medical student, winning the 1908 gold medal.

In September 1928, after being away for a month, Fleming came back to his lab and observed that a culture of *Staphylococcus aureus* he had left out was contaminated. The contamination came from a mold that would come to be known as *Penicillium notatum* (Penicillin). He also discovered that the grape-like colonies of staphylococci surrounding the mold got destroyed.

He describes his discovery this way: "When I woke up just after dawn on September 28, 1928, I certainly didn't plan to revolutionize all medicine by discovering the world's first antibiotic, or bacteria killer. But I suppose that was exactly what I did."

At first, Fleming referred to his discovery as "mould" juice before settling on "penicillin." (named after the mold itself) Fleming investigated further, believing he found an enzyme more powerful than lysozyme. However, it wasn't an enzyme, but one of the first antibiotics.

Fleming preferred to work alone, but penicillin required a team to isolate and purify it. Under the leadership of Howard Florey and Ernst Chain, University of Oxford scientists succeeded in the purification process. The antibiotic got its first use during World War II as medicine for the troops and was later used to control infections.

In 1944, Fleming got knighted, and in 1945 Florey, Chain, and Fleming won the Nobel Prize but could never agree over who deserved the most credit for penicillin. Still, it is generally acknowledged and accepted that Sir Alexander Fleming is the discoverer, if only by accident.

Accidents play a tremendous role in the evolution of the species on Earth. Over six million years, we grew from our apelike ancestors, developing our cerebral cortex, which is vital to human intelligence. Still, It only evolved as a "happy accident" because of our tremendous environmental pressure to survive.

When we think of creative breakthroughs, we usually imagine a person struck by sudden inspiration. We envision a person taking their idea from A to B, but the reality is not that simple. Our creativity doesn't come out of thin air, but it happens in an accident. Fleming left for a month and returned to make his profound discovery.

If we expand our knowledge enough, like Fleming, we will be well-equipped to turn our accidents into advantages. Fleming was expecting a more potent enzyme, but got an antibiotic, unlocking new possibilities to help humanity in creative ways.

Remember this: Never discount the power of accidents. They can be a source of untapped knowledge and creativity. Don't be rigid and close yourself off to new ideas. Instead, be ready to align with the reality of a situation; how you look at the world, and your willingness to adapt will determine the opportunities you see.

Sir Alexander Fleming's Guidance

"I have been trying to point out that in our lives chance may have an astonishing influence and, if I may offer advice to the young laboratory worker, it would be this-never neglect an extraordinary appearance or happening. It may be-usually is, in fact-a false alarm that leads to nothing but may, on the other hand, be the clue provided by fate to lead you to some important advance." – Sir Alexander Fleming

---

Creativity As a System (Alan Turing)

In 1939, Alan Turing accepted a role working in Buckinghamshire at a site called Bletchley Park. Turing worked with the allies on top-secret projects to decipher Axis military codes during World War II. He devoted most of his time at Bletchley Park towards cracking a system known as "Enigma." The Enigma machine encrypted messages, so Axis forces had a protected form of communication.

Polish mathematicians figured out how to read Enigma messages, and shared their information with the British. However, the Germans changed the cipher every day, making it very secure. This daily change erased the codebreaker's efforts the previous day, forcing them to start the decoding process over.

To overcome this puzzle, Turing, along with his colleague Gordon Welchman, invented the machine called the Bombe. The machine's most significant advantage was that it minimized the work of human code-breakers. The Bombe looked within Enigma's internal wheels for keyboard-to-lamp board connection patterns, which decoded letters into plaintext German. Because of The Bombe, the German Air Force messages started getting decoded, helping the Allies use the intelligence to their advantage.

Unlike many before Turing, he also succeeded in decrypting complicated German naval communications. German U-boats plagued the Allies shipping convoys, so intercepting their signals was vital. With captured materials from Enigma, Turing developed "Banburismus," a technique that enabled the reading of enemy naval Enigma messages in 1941.

The "Hut 8" team at Bletchley, performed the cryptanalysis of naval signals from the Germans. Excluding a period in 1942 (when the code was encrypted), the Allied convoys could safely navigate away from German U-boats. Turing's assistance played a crucial position for the Allies in the Battle of the Atlantic.

Alan Turing's feat was a fusion of mathematics and imagination. But, he didn't try to shorthand the complexity of solving the Enigma machine, fitting it into a simple math formula, or statistic. Instead, he worked with his team and thought outside the box. Turing understood that without individual components, "Enigma" couldn't function. So, he looked to the *parts* to understand the *whole*. Once his team solved how the pieces made the machine, he learned the truth of Enigma and built a system (The Bombe) against it.

Consider the different ways you can use your imagination to expand your knowledge and find the truth. Like Turing, reflect on the parts that make the whole. You can use those smaller components to gain an accurate understanding of the big picture, and then design practical solutions to get around your challenges.

Alan Turing's Guidance

"Those who can imagine anything can create the impossible." — Alan Turing

Polarity (Taylor Swift)

Our world has many opposites: light and dark, up and down, forward and backward, left and right. At the same time, there's an abundance of creative material available to those that use these polarities.

Taylor Swift was achieving country music success as a singer/songwriter at 16 years old. She touched country fans with songs such as "You Belong With Me" and "Love Story," which helped her records achieve multi-platinum status.

Fearless (2008), won a Grammy for Album of the Year, and *1989 (*containing "Shake it Off" and "Blank Space") earned Grammys for Album of the Year and Best Pop Vocal Album. *Reputation* (2018) and *Lover* (2019) followed those albums and also reached tremendous success among fans.

By exploring polarities, Swift transforms *feelings* (which are the base material) into music (valuable content). Imagine our emotions being similar to sand. We can go to the desert and find it in abundance. But, how many people can take sand and turn it into something precious? This creative process is the same as transforming a handful of sand into platinum. Let's look at an example of these polarities.

In her hit song "22," Swift captures the feeling of youth and friendship. The music video enhances the narrative as Taylor sings and dances with her most cherished friends. She sings, "We're happy, free, confused, and lonely at the same time. It's miserable and magical." Notice the creativity in the contrast of emotions expressed in the lyrics.

If "22" is about friendship, notice the contrast when compared to her song "The Outside." This song captures the emotions of feeling left out, as though we don't have friends. Many people can relate to feeling as though they don't belong. Swift describes what it's like to be on the outside, with nobody around when she says: "So how can I ever try to be better? Nobody ever lets me in I can still see you, this ain't the best view on the outside looking in."

Polarities are a creation of humans. Nature doesn't distinguish between these dualities, but they do give us a sense of control and an explanation for our surroundings; however, the understanding of reality is more complicated.

From the above example of Swift's songs, you can see that we create concepts such as friendship and isolation. Since they come from our imagination, we have the power to change them whenever we like. For those who don't realize that these concepts are imaginary, they fight against nature's natural order.

On the other hand, think about when we dream. A dream might not make any conscious sense. Still, it combines ideas and experiences into stories that make sense to us in those moments. When we dream of flying hundreds of feet in the sky, our unconscious mind releases the need for polarities, and we're able to combine our imagination and emotions freely.

To unlock your imagination, model Swift, and play with the polarities and contradictions of life. You'll connect with people in a more profound way when you make people aware of their unconscious emotions. What polarities can you see? For instance, people who are kind to others only when it benefits them. Can you feel the edge? The tension in them? These different sides to the same coin contain essential distinctions that can help you develop new and innovative ideas.

Taylor Swift's Guidance

"Never forget the essence of your spark!" — Taylor Swift

Chapter 6: Master Your Purpose

Once we dedicate enough time to a single activity, we reach a higher level of skill, intellect, and understanding. You access this exceptional level of proficiency by devoting your life to your purpose, committing, despite the influences of others. With such devotion, many of the components of your vocation become connected to your unconscious; you can perform without thinking.

Up until this point, you've been *consciously* pursuing and improving yourself at your life's purpose. However, if you want to reach the heights of your abilities, you need the involvement of your *unconscious* mind. With your conscious and unconscious working in sync, you're combining the instinctual strength of animals with the intellectual prowess of humanity. Our brains contain traces of animal and human. We harness both parts by taking what we love and learning it to the point of expertise.

Brooklyn's Jay-Z (Shawn Carter) is a multi-talented force with experience in rapping, writing, and producing music. Originally from the high-crime area of Marcy Projects, rap became his way out; his big break occurred when he debuted his song "The Originators" on *Yo! MTV Raps* in 1989.

Many of Jay's stories are autobiographical, painting pictures of his gritty experiences with drug dealing and violence in the streets. At the start of his career, he called himself "Jazzy," but soon changed it to Jay-Z (after the closeness of the Marcy Projects to subways J and Z).

In 1996, Jay-Z and two friends (Damon Dash & Kareem Burke) founded Roc-A-Fella Records. They released his first album (*Reasonable Doubt*), which topped a million copies sold in the United States. The album featured tracks from big names such as Notorious B.I.G. and Mary J. Blige and peaked at number 23 on the Billboard 200; Jay-Z's rise to fame had begun.

1998 through 2003 was some of Jay-Z's most productive time in his music career. He released a series of successful albums once per year, starting with *Vol. 2: Hard Knock Life* (1998). This album was the first of his collection to top the Billboard 200 chart and earned him the first Grammy of his career for the best rap album.

Even though he was consecutively topping charts, his next milestone came with his 2001 album *The Blueprint*. It received critical acclaim as one of the decade's best albums, making Jay-Z one of hip-hop's most celebrated artists. Even after pleading guilty to assault in a 1999 nightclub stabbing, Jay-Z's career didn't slow down.

Jay-Z surprised the world with his retirement before he released *The Black Album* in 2003. He cited his resignation from the rap game as a lack of competitors by saying, "The game ain't hot, I love when someone makes a hot album and then you've got to make a hot album. I love that. But it ain't hot."

Still, *The Black Album* would be one of his best, with iconic songs such as "99 Problems." A year later, he became president of Def Jam Recordings, standing out as one of the highest-ranking African American executives in the music industry.

A few years later, Jay-Z came out of retirement strong with a new album (*Kingdom Come*). *American Gangster* came a year after, in 2007, and *Blueprint 3* two years later. Jay's sound and purpose changed significantly with these releases because his music incorporated more rock and soul, and the lyrics were less autobiographical. He expressed views on topics such as success, the presidential election, and Hurricane Katrina. At this point in his career, his goal was to express mature views, matching his age. He didn't think older audiences would stay with rap if it didn't express broader views.

More recently, on June 15, 2017, Jay-Z was inducted into the Songwriters Hall of Fame, the first rapper to accomplish this feat. June 30th of that month,

Jay-Z released an exclusive album called *4:44* to his streaming service (Tidal) and Sprint.

The downloads took it to platinum status in less than a week. The album features artists such as Frank Ocean, Beyonce, and Damian Marley, and gained tremendous popularity among fans. Critics celebrated the record for the lyrics and maturity expressed in Jay-Z's music.

Jay's net worth is approximately $1 billion, with business ventures ranging from champagne, art, and real estate in L.A., the Hamptons, and Tribeca. He also has an ownership stake in Uber, and Warren Buffett recommends people learn from him. Understand, most of Jay-Z's breakthrough success occurred in less than a decade.

So, now you're about to learn how you can master your purpose and take your life as far as you can imagine. Your conscious and unconscious mind fuse through habits. When you have the right ones, they will set you free. The only difference between you and someone who has what you want is the habits you apply over time.

To better understand reality, we need to look to nature. Look at the systems and habits it has developed; they're all around us. You can see bears hibernating routinely, fish migrating across the planet predictably, or even the water cycle (evaporation to precipitation). Some of nature's laws include the laws of time, energy, space, matter, and intelligence. We need to align your habits with these laws to get you the maximum positive consequences.

You can choose your habits consciously; however, many people don't. Only humans possess this ability, but we can still take lessons from animals, such as their routines, consistency, and willingness to put in the work to get what they need. Animals don't know what it means to take "a sick day," and they don't know there's a concept such as "quitting."

Therefore, mastering your purpose is, first and foremost, a product of how you *think* about it. One of the most challenging conflicts to overcome is the struggle between us, our thoughts, and our emotions. Your unconscious mind will never give you recommendations on how you should think, but it will take what you feed it and create your reality.

Jay-Z and Buffett spend time together because they understand how vital it is to surround themselves with people who have the right thoughts. Similarly, look at COVID-19, it's been the topic of 2020 because people keep *thinking* and *talking* about the pandemic. As long as people give it attention, it will be a self-fulfilling reality.

So, why are many people financially poor in a flourishing country such as the U.S.? Because poor isn't a condition, it's a mindset. As long as a person thinks, and talks about it, their conscious and unconscious mind will create it.

Remember, in your journey, thinking and acting in a wealthy way is available to us all (for free). Now that you understand *what* you need to master your purpose, let's get practical and understand *how*; the habits you need.

Health

Focusing on our health is priority number one for keeping the mind sharp. Reaching the heights of success in your purpose will mean nothing without the health to savor it. You must be conscious of your health; exercise is a lifestyle developed by habits and the self-discipline to be active.

When your health is taken care of, it feeds your motivation, which further encourages your positive health habits. One is necessary for the other, and we can't do without either if we want to expand our lives and feel fulfilled.

Jay-Z works with his trainer Marco Borges on circuits and cardio that target: shoulders, hips, elbows, and knees. Here's what he has to say: "In continuously striving to be the best, I need to operate with my health in full gear,"

Jay-Z firmly believes that taking care of his physique is also taking care of his mind. For his circuits, he does 3-4 rounds of exercises, doing 12-15 reps. He prefers deadlifts, push-ups, lunges, dumbbell rows, triceps, and cardio on the treadmill.

He also prefers medicine balls and weights and uses them to target those four major joints, instead of muscle groups. He says, "Once you understand how different movements of the joints stimulate different sets of muscles, you can really do anything you want."

Self-Motivation

When we develop self-motivation, it shields you against the destructive effects of procrastination and being lazy. None of these positive habits will matter if you can't motivate yourself to do them every day. Realize that you are the only person that can stimulate your thoughts, and you are the only person that has the control to change your thoughts and actions. Self-motivation is the support you need to inspire you to master your purpose.

Jay-Z had to motivate himself to get out of the Marcy Projects, and he needed to drive himself to wake up every day and continually create new music. You can see this habit best illustrated between 1998 – 2003 when he was dropping platinum and Grammy-winning content year after year, consistently. He got into action and kept moving towards his dreams, billion-dollar dreams.

Vision

Our self-motivation needs to come from somewhere. Nobody is motivated unless they have reasons, and yours is your vision. Vision is who we see ourselves as, and self-motivation is our actions to bridge the gap between who we are in the present and who we see ourselves as in the future.

By getting into the habit of tapping into your creativity, you can reflect on your past-self, and invent new plans for your future. What are you aiming to accomplish? Think of your vision as your mind's eye, which you can tap into for insights that you'll never get in a book.

Recently, Jay-Z and his company Marcy Venture Partners raised $85 million to help startup businesses in the consumer space. In 2016, his vision involved early investments in the future of Uber, Airbnb, and Spotify; however, now he set his sights towards being a venture capital solution for entrepreneurs. Some of the venture capital projects the company is endorsing include a chef service called "Hungry," and an e-bike service called "Wheels."

Focus

When we master our purpose, we're free to choose another calling in our life. A common mistake occurs when people get involved in too many projects at once. Divided attention will never yield exceptional results. However, focusing on a single purpose allows your desire to be written to your unconscious mind. By writing your mission to your unconscious, you start to "print" it into reality.

Focus requires self-discipline, to be willing to say no to most things. Many artists in the music game catch a break and get their first taste of success, but it's often their last. The people that don't last get caught up in the lifestyle. Parties, drugs, and alcohol get the best of them, and they end up back at the beginning. These people come from having little and quickly get everything they ever dreamt of having; it becomes an overload.

Jay-Z didn't come into music with advantages. His careers in business and music exploded at the same time, but he kept his composure. Despite rapping about drinking and partying, he drank moderately and maintained a clear mind, always focused on money and results.

Making these conscious, focused choices, Jay took his initial success and crafted an empire. Model this behavior and always keep a tight focus. Distractions and shiny objects will try to derail you; it's vital to practice keeping your purpose at the center of your attention.

Self-Control

Self-control is vital but only mastered through years of effort and discomfort. It comes from thoughtfully choosing habits and supporting them. Self-control can only grow to the extent of your willpower.

Many people have lost all of their success, life's work, and taken others down with them from a lack of self-control. You can possess all of these habits and still fail to master your purpose from not practicing this particular one.

The most significant benefit to improving our self-control is that we're overcoming one of our most difficult challenges, ourselves.

Jay-Z once said, "I'm not a businessman; I'm a business, man." His self-control comes from looking at himself as a business. We don't need to own a business, to see ourselves as a business. Consider that your words and actions can hurt or help your image, just like a business. If you wouldn't want a news station to report on what you're doing, don't do it.

Practice questioning everything you're doing. Run all of your decisions and actions through a conscious filter. You can always stop yourself, as long as you're operating from a higher self-awareness. Remember, self-control is mostly about increasing your self-awareness.

Failure is Success

Did you know Jay was involved with Chrysler and almost had a Jeep Commander branded after him? The plan was for it to be pre-loaded with his songs, have a butter-cream (leather) interior, and patented Jay-Z blue paint on the outside. Furthermore, Jay would receive royalties up to 10% for each vehicle sale.

The deal meant millions of dollars for Jay-Z, but the Jeep never got produced. Chrysler's management shifted and canceled the arrangement at the last minute. But that wasn't the end of the story.

The deal was a huge blow, and Chrysler's management didn't turn down the idea for the traditional reasons you might think. Chrysler thought his star-power might overshadow the Jeep itself. General Motors had different ideas and hosted a party on the Detroit River with Jay in attendance. Jay-Z showcased his patented blue paint on a GMC Yukon and received a considerable sum of money to attend.

Although a Jay-Z Yukon never emerged on the streets, he used the opportunity to full advantage to market his paint color. Imagine if he gave up after the Chrysler deal fell through. What if he decided to stop trying to pursue deals with the automakers? Jay didn't push harder and put more energy into the Chrysler deal, but he took the failure gracefully and pivoted.

Jay doesn't actively market his failures, but he learns from them. And the knowledge he takes from his failures produces tremendous success. Fail gracefully, learn from your setbacks, come at your problems from a different angle, and find ways to fail more often.

Contrary to what the education system tells people, failure is necessary; it's the blessing that provides wisdom and pays dividends. Taking lessons from setbacks is a habit that you need to practice. You can turn every stumble into a stepping stone and master your purpose by striving to fail the most.

People Help People They Like

Everything in life is a sale. When you're awake, you're selling. Think about when you open your eyes, you need to sell yourself on getting out of bed, right? When we eat our first meal of the day we need to sell ourselves (and our family) to eat healthy as well. We convince ourselves about going to the gym, we persuade others to accept our ideas, and even down to our work, we sell ourselves on not quitting.

Don't be fooled into thinking you're not a salesperson because we all are. It's not a profession; it's a way of life, and to master anything, we need the help of other people. However, other people are far more willing to help the people they like.

Develop the habit of being pleasant to be around by being more agreeable. Contrary to the negative stigma that "yes" people receive, the word *yes* opens doors for you. Think about how you can agree with more people, and ask yourself this, "How can I agree with this person right now?" Or, if you find it hard, "How can I agree with this person's *intentions*?"

When people like you, they're more willing to cooperate and help you get what you want. It might be that contact who introduces you to a top-notch mentor, or the mentor who is ready to go the extra-miles because they believe in you. All of this extra help serves you in mastering your most significant purpose.

When people like you, they think of you more often, and the more attention you get, the more opportunities will flow into your life. Whatever your calling is, it likely requires money and service to others. When your customers like you, you're at the top of their mind when they need what you have. Their return business means added success for you, with less effort. It all stems from giving everyone your best-self every day.

Overdeliver

In everything you do, with everything you are, give far more than you expect to receive. Make a habit of over-delivering in your promises to people, whether it's your business or personal life. If you want to take your purpose as far as you can, This habit will condition you to have a service mindset. This habit is as simple as always giving what you promised, and then giving more on top of that.

Rationality

To master our purpose, we need to make effective decisions. Making the right choices requires us to control our emotions; nobody produces exceptional results when they're emotional. Rational thinking reduces the risk of making easily avoidable errors, impulsive decisions, and guessing. Finally, logical thought will protect you against applying self-motivation in the wrong direction. While self-motivation is vital, it can hurt you if you're motivated by emotional decisions.

Make a habit of questioning your emotional state before you make a decision. Are you calm? Level, and centered? Have you eaten and drank water recently? How was the quality of your last sleep? Are your relationships intact? These factors affect your emotions and reduce your ability to make rational decisions (consciously or unconsciously).

Manage Your Resources

Anyone who fulfills their highest purpose has managed their two essential resources effectively. The most crucial elements you need to control are time and money. Time is vital because we master our mission by disciplining ourselves to devote time to it. Money is necessary because you'll need it to progress to higher levels of your purpose, or you'll want to make more of it by using the skills you've obtained. Your total freedom and liberation depend on the habit of managing these resources.

First, you need to *decide* to get your money and your time right. Jay-Z *decided* a long time ago that he's going to master his purpose, which means he chose to master whatever resources he had. He is self-made and refused to settle for less than he believed he's capable of accomplishing. Settling for less is selfish because you're compromising with life.

Second, get in the habit of doing math. What are your monthly expenses? How much do you need to make doing what fulfills you to cover those bills? How much time do you need to devote to your highest purpose, per day? Week? Month? What are other sources of cash flow do you have that can help you?

Third, always keep your eyes on opportunities to increase your current cash flow. Remember, Jay doesn't just make music; he has investments in businesses, art, sports, casinos, and real estate. He finds opportunities he loves and gets in the habit of mastering them to increase his income. Whatever purpose you want to master, how can you create a new stream of income without any additional effort?

For example, a person gets paid to refer new employees to their company. They make more money, with no additional work. If you're going to master your highest purpose, why wouldn't you increase your income as far as you can?

Fourth, Jay-Z is always considering how an opportunity can financially benefit him. If he's going to give his time to a project, he expects to trade his value for the other parties' money. Jay gave his time to

Chrysler because they were talking about considerable sums of money and assets in return. However, when the Chrysler Jeep deal fell through, Jay went to General Motors (GM) because he knew they wanted to trade their money for his time. Always consider who has your money, and don't give time to people and causes that don't deliver value in return.

Fifth, spend and invest wisely. Remember that everything has an opportunity cost. The money and time we spend could have gone towards something else. For instance, buy a loaf of bread, and you've given up the money, the interest it could have earned, and time that could have gone to making more money.

Jay-Z explains it well in his song "The Story of O.J." He tells how he bought artwork for $1 million; two years later, its worth $2 million, and a few years after, it was worth $8 million. That decision he made with the $1 million could have gone towards something else that left him with less. For example, what if he bought a couple of depreciating Lambos or Rolls Royces? He would have lost the potential $8 million and had a few hundred thousand dollars in cars. Opportunity costs can make or break your life.

Sixth, the most crucial reason for accumulating a surplus of money and time is to invest; Your *time* into your purpose and your money to earn you more freedom. Jay-Z collected his income to put it back into himself. When he sold his albums, he didn't blow it and get himself into a deficit like many artists. He also wasn't scared to take calculated (educated) risks in his investments.

Repeat this procedure and build multiple sources of income for you and your heirs. Consider the legacy behind why you're mastering your purpose. Give your future generations the gift of freedom from the start. You might have to build your wealth and purpose from ground zero. Still, you can make your heirs lives easier by educating them and taking care of the money aspect.

The younger your heirs are when they reach time and financial freedom, the more life they'll have to master the highest purpose of their lives. Giving the gift of total freedom is the most significant contribution you can make to your family.

Contribution

The height of fulfillment in everything you do is contributing to others. If you want to master your highest purpose, adopt the habit of contribution. If you don't feel like you can give 1% of your income or 1% of your time now, then you'll never give 1% of anything when you do have it. The point is to condition yourself to contribute, regardless of how you feel.

Jay started the Shawn Carter Foundation in 2003 to help at-risk youth with scholarships and post-secondary education costs. Since its founding, it has provided millions of dollars to support initiatives that help young people, from rough communities, develop themselves in the world.

As Tony Robbins says, "The secret to living is giving." All of the success in the world is meaningless without paying it forward, serving others, and helping them achieve what fulfills them. Practice these habits, and they will serve you for a lifetime, teach them to your family, and they will serve as your legacy.

Jay-Z's Guidance

If the beat is time, flow is what we do with that time, how we live through it. The beat is everywhere, but every life has to find its own flow. - Jay-Z

Bonus Chapter: *You Are Free*

Chapter 1: Understand Your Freedom

"**Truth** - *more precisely, an accurate understanding of* **reality**- *is the essential foundation for* *producing good outcomes." – Ray Dalio*

---

9 a.m. / Marlin's Park in Miami

Over 20,000 people roar, while AC/DC's "Thunderstruck" pulses through every inch of the park. The stadium wasn't roaring for a baseball game, but a business conference. We looked into the sky and saw the head of the conference drifting in by parachute. He sky-dived into Marlin's park. The head of the conference is a multi-million dollar icon who came from rock-bottom to the pinnacles of wealth.

He's built a real estate empire with over $1 billion in assets under management. He has spoken in many countries about wealth, success, and legacy.

To get what he has, he spent more than 30 years of his life doing things he hated. He explained the long hours, massive stress, and endless days on the road (at his expense) to get in front of people he didn't like. His life has become a collection of things, Rolls Royces and private jets, but that day, you could tell in his face that he was exhausted.

He had all of the empty bragging rights, flashed the cash, and emphasized the importance of getting ridiculously wealthy. The conference stressed that your success is equal to your income. However, I didn't want to spend the next 30 years of my life grinding for cash, just for cash's sake. I wanted the money and lifestyle. I think *both*, not *either/or*, and I refused to believe I had to give up one to have the other.

The speaker was alive outside but dead inside. And don't get me wrong, this icon is healthy, wealthy, has a great family, and appears to have a fulfilled life. However, it took over 30 years and a lot of pain. He admitted during these 30 years that he didn't go out to eat, rarely took a vacation, and traveled just to speak over 300 days of the year.

Wasting years to live finally is where we don't want to end up.

The Sheep vs. The Black Sheep

What are the glaring differences between *sheep* and the *black sheep* who dare to think differently? It's priorities. The usual response to life is to work hard, sacrifice, and save for retirement. When *sheep* finally retire, they collect social security and budget their life's savings. Their goal is to make their money last until they die, and "if" they're lucky, take a couple of vacations, and leave a little for their children.

The priorities of the rare *black sheep* involve time. These are people who don't believe in the word "retirement." The *black sheep* think it's ridiculous to lose years of your life to live someday later. The *black sheep* understand that they're not a one-person show; their freedom comes from employing other people to do the work they don't want to do.

When the *black sheep* want to do something, they do it, and always make themselves more important than their work. Leverage is key to getting the most done, with the least amount of effort. You can leverage other people, technology, or money to take back your time. Once you take back your time, you can devote it to making more money, which further allows you to leverage more people, giving you more time.

Sheep want to make money to buy stuff. The *black sheep* desire experiences, realizing that more *things* won't fulfill them. They understand that fulfillment comes from time spent in a meaningful way. To make more money, *sheep* want to climb the ladder and become the boss. However, the *black sheep* don't care about titles or positions; they care about control. The *black sheep* want to feel in control of their life, with the command to do what they want when they want while earning a ton of money to do it.

Most of the *sheep* around us want to have more things, just to accumulate. There's nothing wrong with wanting more; the *black sheep* also want more. However, these rare people realize that they get more by having less. To experience a free life, don't chain yourself to material things. Sure, some things are necessary, and some things we want, but most people have too much. What we want more of in our lives is quality. Seek more quality and less congestion. You put new additions on your home and decorated it with all new furniture, but what purpose are you serving that's bigger than you? What fulfills you? Are you helping to uplift other people, or are you doing meaningless work that you hate every day?

Most *sheep* are working towards a golden payoff on the other side, whether it's retirement, a pension (rare), a buyout, inheritance, or some large sum of money. Everyone needs to think big, but focus in on the present. Focus on cash-flow, getting paid every day, from multiple streams. Think of it as the golden goose vs. the golden egg. The golden egg is where most people put their attention. These are the people who max out their 401k's and IRA's to accumulate a considerable nest egg. Then, retirement comes around, and they start drawing from these funds, trying to make them last. Slowly, the golden egg starts to get smaller and smaller.

On the other hand, the golden goose lays the golden eggs; the golden goose is cash-flow. Would you rather have $2 million in a retirement account that you can't touch or $150,000 per year for the rest of your life? Don't build a golden egg, create a golden goose to lay your golden eggs; I'll show you how later in the book.

Finally, *sheep* want freedom from the things they don't enjoy. The *black sheep* also want this freedom. The difference is that *sheep* don't have a reason for wanting the freedom they desire. If they had it, they would find creative ways to waste it. But, the *black sheep* want the freedom to pursue their passions in life. These people don't want to stop contributing to society; they want to stop providing to causes that don't matter to them; they want their contributions to feel meaningful. While the *sheep* work, just to work, it's for paycheck, not purpose. Whatever you're contributing to society right now, whatever you do for work, would you do it for free? Imagine if all of the benefits got stripped away, and all that was left was you and your profession. Would you be as enthusiastic every day to get up and get it done? If not, then you're not pursuing and experiencing the full impact of this planet. We're going to change that!

The Rat Race

People stuck in the rat race are playing the game to pay bills—those who want more from life desire to beat the rat race. Beating the game means you're not playing to pay bills anymore. Early in my life, I noticed my mom was always looking for someone to pay (whether she realized it or not). Whenever she received an inflow of money, everyone got paid, except us.

Have you looked at the rules of your expenses? Companies have policies in place for payments, late payments, grace periods, and promotions. Often, paying bills isn't as black and white as we think. What if you had a grace period where you didn't have to pay someone for five days after the due date? And, what if that grace period came with no fees? You could defer paying someone for five days and use that money to generate more money. Always pay on-time at the last possible moment.

Take credit cards; for example, it's no secret they come with some mean interest rates. But they also come with some sweet rewards. At the time of this writing, the world is wrestling with COVID-19, which has opened up tremendous opportunities as companies try to evolve and accommodate their customers. Many payment processing companies, such as Yardi, are waiving transaction fees for credit card payments. My wife and I use a credit card to pay rent on an app. Doing it this way has three massive benefits:

First, it defers the rent payment to the next month, freeing the cash to pay yourself instead.

Second, it gives considerable cash back credit card rewards. Who doesn't want the credit card company to pay 5% of your expenses every month?

Third, you can drop the cashback reward in a tax-free investment vehicle. The credit card companies are giving you free money to fund your lifestyle.

Want another example? Did you know that you can use life insurance to self-insure yourself for car insurance? That money every month that pours out of your account to the car insurance company can be flowing back into your account. You can pay yourself every month, the same money you would have paid to the car insurance company, while still having car insurance. How would you like to be your own car insurance company and make the money they make off you every month, with returns? I'll leave everything in the resources section.

Is it unethical to use the established rules to our advantage? No, because they're there to use. Aside from laws and science, everything can be reformed and shaped. Evolution occurs when people stop doing things the way they always have. Your lifestyle will transform when you challenge the current order and use the rules to give yourself more freedom.

Challenging the Current Order (The Right Way)

If it's not broken, don't fix it. It's essential to be different when something isn't working. However, it's senseless to try to reinvent the wheel. Are you familiar with the story of the ham pan?

The story of the ham pan is about four people; let's call them Jen, Katie, Molly, and Cathy; all related as mothers and daughters.

Jen's the youngest. Katie's Jen's mother. Molly's Jen's grandmother, and Cathy's Jen's great-grandmother. Jen recently married a great guy named Mike.

Their family is traditional because they love to put together big holiday dinners for Thanksgiving and Christmas. Turkey on Thanksgiving, and then usually turkey or roast duck for Christmas.

Katie and Jen have always done the holidays this way. It's also the way Molly learned to do the holidays from her mom, Cathy. Last year was Jen's first year preparing the traditional meal with Mike.

This family has another beautiful tradition. Each prepares a delicious baked ham in December, for a feast in their family households.

Jen makes a ham; so does Katie, Molly, and Cathy. They all prepare it in the same way with a unique glaze.

Then they cut off the end of the ham, toss it out, place the remaining meat into the pan and pour the glaze over it. It roasts at 350 degrees for 2 ½ hours and its ready to eat.

Jen and Mike were newlyweds last year, learning about each other's family traditions. As Mike was in the kitchen, helping Jen prepare the ham, he noticed she cut the end of the meat off and threw it away. Naturally, he was curious about this and asked, "Jen, why do you cut the end of the ham off and throw it away? It looks good to eat!"

Jen replied, "I don't know. My mom always did it that way, so that's how I do it."

That answer wasn't enough for Mike because he thought it was a waste of food. So he asked Jen to ask her mom why the ham has to have the end cut off before it goes into the oven.

Jen finished up in the kitchen, called her mom, and asked, "Mom, why do you cut the end of the ham off and throw it away before putting the ham into the oven?"

Katie replied, "I'm not sure, that's the way my mom did it, so I always do it that way too. And over the years, I have thrown away a lot of ham. But you know what? I'll call and ask grandma the reason."

They hung up, and Katie called her Mom, Molly, to ask why she always cuts the end of the ham off and throws it away.

Molly thought about it for a minute and answered, "I don't know, my mom did it whenever she was making the ham. Now that I think about it, I've thrown away a lot of ham over the years. This situation has me thinking, so I'm going to call her up and ask why we always cut off the end of the ham."

So Molly hung up with Katie and called her mom, Cathy. Molly tells Cathy that her, Jen, and Katie were wondering why they're supposed to cut off the end of the ham. Molly tells her that between the four of us, we have thrown a lot of food away.

Cathy thinks for a minute and then says. "I don't know why you, Katie, and Jen cut off the end of the ham and throw it away, but I do it because my ham roasting pan is so small. The ham won't fit any other way."

Some of the things we learn are very helpful when we're young. But the truth is that when we're little, everything our parents do is the "right way." We do some things because we don't know any other way to do them. If the people around us are doing it that way, it must be the way we are supposed to do it. Right?

We adopt ideas and actions from others that seem harmless because (for the most part) people are passing along what they know to be "the right way." If those ideas serve you now, keep them, and if they don't, let them go. Removing what doesn't help you is how you challenge the current order (the right way).

There's no need to hold old ideas that don't work, don't elevate your life, and hurt you. Stop throwing the ends of your ham away just because you saw someone else do it. If you want something different, be a different person. When you think differently, you'll feel differently.

You control your life, and nobody will ever care about it more than you.

Keep the following principles in mind as you progress through the book. These principles are the common "sacred cows" that many people still hold for no reason.

All stress is bad stress. When we feel pressured, it isn't always bad. Good stress elevates us to new heights because it urges us to rise above challenges. In your journey to increase your freedom, the goal isn't to kill *all* stress from your life. We need to bring more good pressure into your life while killing the bad. Harmful stresses weaken you, make you less capable, and rob you of your best performance. These pressures include things such as bullying, abuse, harassment, toxic environments, and our weaknesses; these have to go.

Good stress is incredible! Examples include mentors who push us, training in the gym, solving problems, and educating ourselves. When we feel the edge of our comfort zone, we're also in an excellent stress zone. The more positive pressure you place on yourself, the faster you can take back your life and experience freedom from the negative.

The freest people are the ones that actively kill negative stress while embracing positive pressure.

Money is the only currency. Most people think in terms of dollars per hour, cash per month, and salary per year. To take back more of your freedom, realize you don't need to make more money than everyone else. You can make half the money of another person and still be wealthier than them. You can have more wealth with less money because money is only one of two currencies. Often, people forget that we measure wealth in *time,* the second form of currency. Let me show you:

Let's use an example with two people, Tom and Cindy. Tom earns $100,000 per year and works 50 hours per week in an office; at a job, he can't stand. Cindy earns $50,000 and works 20 hours per week; she also can't tolerate her career. When Tom isn't working, he loves going fishing on Lake Michigan; Tom tries to get out at least 20 hours a week. Cindy's a dancer in her spare time who loves lyrical dance. Cindy is in the dance studio practicing for performances at least 30 hours per week. Who's richer?

If the world ran only in terms of dollars, it would be Tom, of course. But Tom spends 30 *more* hours in the office than Cindy, to earn $100,000. There are 52 weeks in a year, and Tom is working 50 hours every week. That comes out to **$38** an hour for Tom's time.

Cindy works 30 *fewer* hours than Tom and makes half the income. Still, with 52 weeks in the year and Cindy working 20 per week, Cindy's time is worth **$48** per hour. Also, Cindy spends ten more hours than Tom doing what she loves, and she could easily add more time to it because she's only using 50 hours per week with dance and work.

Tom, on the other hand, is already at 70 hours per week, between work and fishing. And more than half of his time is going towards something he doesn't enjoy. When Tom does have a few moments, he gets away and finally enjoys his life before the reality of his work strikes again. Does this sound familiar?

Our goal is to ratchet up your income while reducing your working time. We can manipulate the two currencies -time and money- to increase your freedom and mobility. Later in the book, we're going to figure out the minimum amount you need per hour (with the least amount of hours) to set you free.

Money is not an excuse. So many distract themselves with money and work. Money and work are two convenient excuses to avoid doing the things we want. How many times have you heard people say they don't have the money or can't get the time off work? These people think that once they reach a particular promotion, or once they hit a specific dollar amount, they'll "arrive" and finally begin living. They never do.

Letting money and work take our time is the easiest way to avoid pursuing the life we want. "Michelle, we'd love to go on that Aspen trip with you and Roger, but I have this massive project at work! I don't know how I'll get it done in the next five days; I've been going into work three hours early just to answer 200 unnecessary emails." Or, "Michelle, I don't know how we could ever afford to go to Aspen, I didn't get that promotion and yearly bonuses haven't come in."

Everyone is playing the same game, staying busy, distracting themselves with money and work. As you can see, the problem is more than money. The challenge is that people's routines are easy excuses to avoid the discomfort of doing something different. Instead of asking, "how can I make this happen?" many tell themselves, "I can't make this happen." This subtle difference is devastating.

Take everything in moderation. When you have too much of anything, it becomes poisonous. This excess even includes essentials such as water, clothing, food, and time. When we design your free life, we're not aiming for a surplus of *free* time, but instead, an excess of time you can apply to the things that make you feel fulfilled. More time doing what you love, less time doing what you think you *have* to do

Remember, too much of a positive almost always creates a negative.

Focus on your strengths and outsource your weaknesses. One of the most significant flaws in our education system is the emphasis on being well-rounded. You don't need "General Education," you need to master your strengths. The fact is, there are more things we're terrible at, than talented. This world has far too many different directions we can go, and there's no way we can master all skills and abilities in a lifetime.

So, would you rather be mediocre at many things, or master a couple? Few things sap our confidence more than trying to improve our weaknesses. What's the point, when someone in the world is exceptional where you're weak already; delegate it to them. By only focusing on your strengths, you're applying your time towards your advantages, and you can use your abilities to give you more time freedom.

When I was in business school, I struggled my way through math. The x's and y's made no sense to me. At that point, I was already operating a successful investment portfolio of consumer loans that paid me passive income daily. I thought to myself, "why do they teach people in business calculus?" Success in finances only requires basic math.

It's more fun, more productive, and more prosperous to focus all of your attention on your areas of strength. Mastering one of your advantages can set you free, because that strength is someone else's weakness, and they'll pay you for it.

Don't ask if you can "do," and don't apologize too often. Your time is *your* time. Your life is *your* life. To have more freedom in your life, you need to begin acting free. Here are two surefire ways to spot a person who submits themselves to others:

They ask for permission all the time, and they apologize for their existence. If you want to do something for yourself that isn't hurting you or others, do it. If you ask for permission to do it, people default to "no" more often than "yes."However, if you do it without asking, people are much *less* likely to step in your way and stop you. Are you having a hard time getting what you want from life? It might be because you need to stop asking for permission. It's much better to take responsibility for taking action than letting others decide your life.

Apologizing too often is a meaningless habit that diminishes your value to others. To increase the freedom in your life, you need to be bold and unapologetic for who you are. Always take responsibility for your actions, and own your mistakes, but never apologize for being yourself.

You didn't find that answer at work for someone? Don't apologize. Are you having a bad hair day? Don't say sorry for it. Did you have to leave work early to take care of something in your personal life? You're not sorry. Were you a few minutes late to a party? Sorry, not sorry. If we're not conscious, we apologize many times a day, unconsciously.

Nobody wants to hear, "I'm sorry." People want you to demonstrate that you carry yourself with dignity. The people with the most freedom and mobility own who they are, show strength, express courage, and don't apologize for their existence. Do you want more freedom and flexibility in your life? You now know what to do and what not to do.

"Perfect" timing. Once upon a time, I worked for one of the largest real estate lenders in the United States. The company had me working 80 hours per week, with at least two *mandatory* Saturdays a month. The company had a robust auto-dialer system, where I would make at least 500 – 700 outbound calls per day to sell people on refinancing their homes. The money was a couple of hundred grand per year in commissions, but hearing the word "NO" a couple of hundred times a day, six days a week is exhausting.

I wanted to walk away from the job, but the money kept drawing me in. Every day I told myself, "I'll quit someday soon, I just need to make a little more money and make a few more sales." The problem with "someday" is that it never comes. I was waiting for the perfect moment to step away from a job that was making me ill.

The perfect moment will never come for you either. If you want something, or you don't want something in your life, you need to fire first and aim after. Nothing is ever as complicated as we see it in our head, and often, it doesn't turn out how we think it will. That's because we can't tell the future, we just make assumptions about how we think it will go. If you can foresee the future, please go and win the lottery.

One morning, I summoned the courage to walk into my Vice President's office and quit that job in real estate. Not only did I leave, but I also didn't give them two weeks notice, I just left. As I walked out the door for the last time, there was a rush of emotions. It was 10 a.m., and I felt free, completely liberated, and joyous! I was downtown, and everyone was rushing, on their phones, utterly blind to the beautiful day around them. That was the moment I realized that the world is a lot less crowded when we make different decisions. Everyone else was chained to their desk, settling for some PTO and dreaming of 5 p.m. However, I was with my loved ones, planning a trip to Hawaii for the first time. Little did I know I would live there three years later.

I'm writing this book for you, from my pristine 3rd story loft in Kapolei, Hawaii. It's a gorgeous morning, just like every morning. Our view is a town called Makakilo, gently nestled into the hill. It reminds me that this reality almost didn't come to be. The perfect moment will never arrive, and you'll take that "someday" thinking to the grave. Whatever it is you want to do, do it. When you do, you'll wonder why you were ever scared of living your dreams.

Less is more. Doing less work doesn't make people lazy slackers. Many jobs come with a lot of fat (minutiae) that needs trimming. Busy work is a great way for people to look productive while hiding and collecting a paycheck. When we get down to the meat of it, our only job is to serve people. We all have internal and external customers who rely on us. If the work we're doing isn't directly benefiting them, it's busywork.

Keep this in mind as you work, because you'll realize that you can cut away much of your work; saving you time and increasing your freedom to do what's important to you. Take writing a book, for example; what if the writer kept pushing off writing the book? What if a writer obsessed over marketing research, logo's, brand, and social media business pages, but never *wrote* the book? Writing the book is directly beneficial to serving people. If the author doesn't write the book, none of the other things matter.

Now, imagine the author writes the book and outsources everything else (the minutiae). The author is free and flexible to devote time to anything that fulfills them. You're the author of your life. Do what's necessary, what writes the book, and delegate, eliminate, or outsource the minutiae. You're doing less, and receiving more. I'll show you how later in the book.

You need time off. As mentioned earlier, the majority of people are trying to hoard their enjoyment for retirement. However, it's critical to pepper in time off for recovery, more than a couple weeks per year. Our energy fluctuates based on how interested we are and how often we're doing something. One of our core human needs is variety. Variety introduces energy, recovery, and increases our performance.

When you increase your time off, you're ensuring you only work when you're going to be highly productive. The goal is to get you to a point where you take off one week for yourself, for every two weeks of production for others.

What's the point in waiting until a time when our most capable years have passed, to finally enjoy life? One of my mentors once told me, "If people knew what it feels like to be old, they'd prepare when they're younger." Preparation means time off for recovery. You can do it; anyone can do it, as soon as they decide.

Retirement is bad. The idea of retirement is that a person will one day be able to stop working and start living. By this definition, a person who dreams of retiring doesn't like the work they do already. If a person doesn't like the work they do and still does it, it means they feel like they don't have a choice. Since these people don't think they have options, they don't have freedom.

Trying to save for retirement doesn't work for most mathematically. Many financial planners claim that people will be in a lower tax bracket when they retire. However, that's because they base it on the assumption that people will draw less money from their retirement account than they were making at work. Do you want to make less money when you're older? I don't. Do you want to live on hot dogs for dinner? I don't. Besides trying to live on "The Golden Egg" of a 401k, or IRA, inflation reduces purchasing power by at least 2% per year. On top of inflation, taxes must increase in the future. Between the trillion-dollar deficit and unfunded liabilities of the government, the money can only come from one source: taxpayers. Finally, 401k's and IRA's are *exceptions* to the government's rules for taxes. Don't you find it suspicious that the government would make an *exception* to their tax laws, instead of just changing the tax laws? Millions of people are in this boat, working as long as they can because they're scared of running out of money in their golden years. So let's get off this boat

One more thing, some people are incredibly hard-working and diligent. They make retirement happen and accumulate enough to live decently and enjoy their later years. For those that worked so hard to retire finally, a couple of weeks into retirement, they often get so bored with their newfound freedom that they go out and find work to keep them active. So, if you're in this camp, and put in extra effort to retire, isn't the purpose of those years of work defeated, if you're working again?

Retirement isn't our goal, because to retire is to admit that you don't like what you do now. Our goal is to help you live a free life now. Retirement won't matter because nobody wants to stop doing the things they love, the things that make us feel fulfilled. Look at

Warren Buffett; retirement isn't a thing for Warren because he already loves what he does.

Prepare for the future, but instead think of your preparation as a hedge that protects you if (someday) you can't physically do what you love anymore. Don't think of it as a reservoir of cash to eventually enjoy your life.

Reflection A

- How has being a "responsible adult" kept you from doing what you want in your life?
- How has doing what everyone says you should, brought you a life that's less than you want?
- Do the people around you have the life you want? What future will you have if you keep following the same path as everyone else? When we do what others do, we get what others get. How would your future change if you did things differently than the people around you?

The Elephants Rope

Walking through an elephant camp, James noticed a small rope that secured the adult elephants by their ankle. James was curious why the elephants didn't just break the line and go free. He asked the trainer, Daniel, why the small rope kept the elephants secured. Daniel told James that each elephant had the same size rope attached to their ankle when they were babies. When the baby elephants couldn't break free, they grew into adults that believe the line is too strong to break free.

The elephants learned to be helpless from a young age. When we don't believe we can avoid or stop the discomforts in our lives, we stop trying to do anything about it, even if we have chances to escape. This phenomenon happens when we *assume* we can't do something because we failed at it in the past. Limiting beliefs kill breakthroughs, and there's no shortage of people who will tell you the things you can't do. You can learn from the past, you can break free, and you can grow as soon as you let go of your limiting beliefs; your "small" rope.

Living in Hawaii, there's no shortage of tourists. One of our favorite spots is a little resort town on the west side of Oahu called Ko'Olina. As we enjoy the walking trails and lagoons, we always meet a handful of timeshare members enjoying their two-week getaway. Tourists often assume that my wife and I are tourists because we're there, and they're usually surprised to find out that Hawaii is our home.

Ordinarily, their responses are always similar: "I would LOVE to live in Hawaii! It's heaven on Earth, but I just can't because I (insert excuse). The most common reasons we hear are: it's too expensive, they can't leave their work back home, they have a house, cars, or kids and they're stuck. My wife and I smile because we know they'll leave the island, go back home, fall into the same routines, and dream of their two-week vacation next year.

That's the life that many have accepted. Once upon a time, these people had ambitions, but they stopped trying. These people agree to put in for approval to have a few weeks of their life back every year. They go somewhere or do some things that help them temporarily forget the dull reality waiting for them back home. Ordinary people sit on social media and watch everyone else live their lives while doing nothing with their own. Then, these same people get jealous of other's successes and call it *luck*. I won't let you tie that small rope around your ankle.

Using Negativity To Your Advantage

Whatever you're scared to do, I want you to imagine the worst that can happen if you did it. Then, write down those things that could occur, whatever comes to your mind, write it down. Next to each item you write, be honest with yourself, and rate it on a 1-10 scale for how much it would damage your life. A one is minor, and ten is a meltdown. Repeat this until you can't come up with any more negative scenarios.

Ever since I was little, I admired the US military. Growing up in Michigan, the military presence is far less than many other states. Still, I adored a small base near my home called Selfridge. Once a year, the Blue Angels would soar through the sky's of Selfridge, challenging gravity, and mesmerizing the crowd. It was the strength, precision, and discipline that attracted me to the military.

What's crazy is that our family has almost no military background. Other than my grandfather being a merchant marine, we didn't come from any long line of service members. But, at the beginning of 2015, that was all about to change. That was the year I knew I needed to escape Michigan.

Do you know people who will give their last dollar to help their family? Even if it means hurting themselves? That was me. My mom gets one small social security check per month, and I was working hard to be a loyal son who contributes to the family financially. I thought that it was my duty to do whatever I could to help my family. But, I needed to take the most challenging act of my life and take my financial independence.

What I'm about to tell you is difficult for a lot of people to swallow. It goes against our ingrained loyalty to our families. Here it is: to help anyone financially, we need to help ourselves first. From personal experience and numerous observations, those that commit to financially helping their immediate family, regularly, without helping themselves first, end up broke like them.

The Army recruiter got me set up to leave for basic training in August 2015. I was frightened and remembered wondering how my family members would survive financially. I thought they were going to end up homeless and unable to live without me. Funny, it's been five years as of this writing, they quickly got used to me leaving, and they never ask for anything.

What's funny is that on a scale of 1-10, my problems were (at most) a 4. In my head, I made them out to be a ten and almost talked myself out of the level

10 life my wife and I live in Hawaii. As I wrote out my worst fears, I started to think of solutions *if* the situation occurred. My mind switched from *problems* to *solutions*. Back then, I always had the option to go back to Michigan after the Army, get another job, work hard, and give my family money, all with no extra effort.

Here's what this means for you: Your problems are (likely) smaller in reality than they are in your head. There's a level 10 life waiting for you, and you're letting level 4 problems hold you back. You can always go back to how you used to live if you try something new, and it doesn't work. This combination means you have a massive potential gain from doing what you want, and no risk if it doesn't work.

I purchased two one-way tickets to Hawaii, none of our disasters happened, and we continue to live happily ever after. We continue to take care of our financials so that we can take care of the people we love the right way, instead of becoming another charity case.

There are two ways to approach helping anyone: *Enabling* them or *empowering* them. Enabling others makes them dependent on you. No matter how much you give, it's an endless hole where people will want more from you. When a person is enabled enough, they develop new expectations. At first, giving them $10 was enough. Then, they start to ask for $20, $30, $50, and more. Most forget gratitude and begin to feel entitled. The people who do this for people are giving the fish, instead of teaching to fish.

When you empower people, you *teach* them to sustain themselves. People who just want a handout hate this because they love the easy route. Those people never challenge themselves, and they don't want to start now. Think of it this way, if you could choose to have Serena Williams tennis racket or Serena Williams tennis skills, which would you take?

You're giving people the *skills* to hit, not the equipment. Equipment gets stolen, but nobody can take abilities and knowledge. *Empower* the people you love, and show them how to prosper in life, instead of setting them up for failure by enabling.

Fear Likes To Hide

Does fear come right out and show itself as fear? Nope. We give it other names and mold it to our situations. Negative and positive people mask their fear, and it's not until many get backed into a corner that they finally act.

Let's start with negative people. When negative people are scared, they dress up fear with clever justifications. For instance, "What's the point in me trying to get that promotion? Jennie's just going to get it anyway."

Positive people justify fear differently. When positive people are scared, they say things such as: "I don't need to get that promotion. There will be plenty of opportunities in the future because this company is great."

When our work is dull and draining, we can convince ourselves of different realities to help cope. The biggest mistake with fear is that many people think it will get better or go away with more money or time. For example, "If I just had more time with my family, we'd take that trip to Santorini."

You won't wake up one day and have your life just improve itself. Do you think it will? If you have to think about that question, you've been fooling yourself.

How has your life changed tremendously from a year ago? A month ago? A week ago? If it hasn't changed much, it won't change until you change. Would you like to know the cure? Choose something you want to do and do it. Pick something (large or small) that you've always wanted to experience. Whatever you choose, you're on the right track when your mind starts telling you all the reasons you *can't* do it. Whatever it is, facing that fear is your path to liberation.

Reflection B

Write out your answers to the following questions without thinking about it. Whatever comes to your mind, write it—no holding back, there are no wrong answers. Writing out these answers will serve you in overcoming your fear of doing.

What do you want to do, but haven't because of fear? How many uncomfortable situations have you put yourself in lately? Our success rises in proportion to our comfort level. When we have expectations about the way a scene will go, it's easy for us to scare ourselves by making up an outcome. "If I talk to my manager about *that*, I know what he's going to say." No, you don't, because nobody can predict the future. We don't know what will happen because the outcome has *never* happened in reality.

What are you giving up by not doing what you want? What is the opportunity cost in terms of your health, your wealth, your spirituality, and your emotions? The next 5 and 10 years are going to pass anyway. If you look out five years and don't do what excites you, what makes you feel free, where will your life be? What will not taking the actions you desire cost in 10 years? Your most significant risk isn't what you imagine; it's that time will pass by as you live a life of regret.

What's taking so long to do what you want? If you're waiting for the perfect moment, you're scared. The rest of the world shares that feeling with you. However, how much time has inaction cost you already? How much more time will it need to cost before enough is enough? The most critical success habit of those living free and fulfilling lives is action; they jumped first and then figured it out.

What is your worst-case scenario for doing what you want? Write out those "what if" scenarios that flood into your mind. Visualize them as vividly as you can, feel it, taste it, smell it, hear it. Would your worst-case scenario mean death, permanent damage, and would it even matter in 20 years? What's the likelihood of your worst-case scenario occurring?

How can you solve your worst-case scenario if it occurs? Once you settle your worst-case scenario, there's nothing left to stop you. You've slain the "leader" of your fearful thoughts, the biggest dragon. Everything else after seems like child's play. Many times, the worst-case has a bigger *bark* than *bite*. How would you take control of the situation and solve it if it happened?

What are the more likely situations that will occur, and how will they benefit you? Since you know the worst-case, and you developed a plan to solve it, what are the best-case scenarios? How impactful would the best-cases be on your life? How will the best-case situations matter in 20 years? Who has or does what you want? Are they less intelligent than you?

If you lost all of your sources of income today, how would you recover? Imagine if you dropped all of the work that's wasting your time to pursue your dreams. How easily could you go back to the life you have now? If you need to, how quickly and easily could you slide back into your current work? If you returned, how would your experience doing what you want, build you into a more valuable person that commands more income? Remember, no one can take away your skills, abilities, knowledge, and wisdom.

The Pistons vs. The 76'ers

January 31st, 2014, I settle into my cushy leather seat, just feet from Andre Drummond, swish, swish. The Pistons were squaring off against the Sixers in Detroit, and I had courtside seats. I've been obsessed with basketball since I was a young boy. How could I not be? I grew up watching Michael Jordan in his prime. But we were poor when I was young, and I'd be lucky if we had a seat in the nosebleeds.

I got courtside seats because I decided to take a *jump*. It wasn't my first Piston's game, but it was the only one that mattered. As I looked out over the arena, it was almost empty. How crazy is that? Courtside seats came with early entry, so it was mostly me, the player's family, the players, and essential personnel.

As I looked out at the arena, it struck me that 24,000 people would pack in, all with the same plan, there for the same reasons, but only about 30 of us would truly experience the game. If you've never had that kind of access to an event, it's like experiencing an entirely different world.

Do you know what's interesting? I know many thousands of people were looking down on us, wishing they could be in our seats, and any of them could have. The tickets were publicly available online, for anyone to have. All they had to do was pay a little bit more. But they didn't.

The moral is that it's *very crowded* when you do ordinary things, and *very uncrowded* when you rise above. To rise above the average, you only need to give a little more than you already do, because most people won't. These people believe they're acting in *reality*.

Being *realistic* makes for a challenging life. However, being *unrealistic* makes life simple and less competitive. It was simple to get the courtside seat, get in the arena early, beat the lines, have a waiter serve my food, and mingle with a couple of people around me. It's challenging to arrive with everyone else, wait outside in winter, find your seat among thousands, miss part of the game for snacks, and sit around obnoxious fans.

This example is only one of many. What separates these experiences? Nothing except a couple of hundred dollars. However, so many convince themselves that courtside seats and the best things in life are *unrealistic*. As though the best of life is only for the 1%. It's not true!

Aim for grand slams while the rest of the world goes for base hits; big goals have less competition and give you more freedom.

That night we all shared in the Pistons win, but few ate filet mignon, drank excellent wine, danced with Hooper (the mascot), and were so close that a Pistons player fell on them. Everyone left with *memories,* but almost none left with a priceless experience. Nothing beats living your dreams in an *"unrealistic"* life!

What Stimulates You?

Most people are asking themselves vague questions, and life's giving them vague answers. A lot of people ask themselves, "what do I want?" However, that question is way too broad to get a useful solution. When we decide what we want and what our goals are, we're choosing what *stimulates* us. You're selecting a target for the *stimulation* you believe it will bring you.

When you think about your passions, your desires, your bliss, it's all referring to the same thing: stimulation. You want to feel excited. The opposite of feeling stimulated is feeling bored. Have you ever sat through a PowerPoint presentation that you thought would never end? Or a project that was repetitive and tedious?

Stop asking yourself, "what do I want," or "what are my goals?" Instead, ask, "what stimulates me?" Your happiness will come from your level of stimulation. This exciting feeling is your real objective. Nobody wants to do the things that bore them willingly, and all the freedom in the world won't matter if you're bored.

Again, what stimulates you? Let your instincts draw you towards it; don't think about it; just do it more often.

You Need More Than Work

Have you ever told yourself, "when I reach **X** goal, then I'll do **Y**!" For example, "when I get $100,000 in the bank, then I'll start living!" When we aren't *specific* with **Y**, we use **X** to procrastinate. When I worked for a real estate company, I'd tell myself every day that once I reach the "President's Club" in sales, I'll start traveling.

When we're little, we have incredible dreams. Limits don't exist, and anything is possible. Some of us have people who encourage us to become any person we want. On the other hand, many kids don't because the people in their life squash their dreams. Many little kids get told by the people in their environment to quit dreaming and be *realistic*.

So, what do these children do? They grow up and work hard to be *realistic*. Being *realistic* involves soul-crushing work and clever rationalizations to convince themselves that everything will work out. Then, they have children, pass down the same harmful information, and the cycle continues.

The challenge is that we focus on **X** and neglect **Y**. In other words, we can focus so hard on reaching a goal (**X**) that we have no idea what we'll do with ourselves after we reach the goal (**Y**). This lack of *"unrealistic"* dreams is why people reach goals and then start working towards the next goal, never giving themselves the freedom to have what they want.

You need more than work; you need dreams that stimulate you. When you have exciting ideas, you don't keep cycling back to **X** and working yourself to death. You can spot the people that *don't* have this figured out because they look successful on the outside. They have beautiful cars, beautiful homes, nice jobs, and excellent businesses. But they're dead inside, they're miserable, and don't know why. It's because they never allow themselves to do stimulating activities away from work.

Grey Hairs And Timeshares

When I worked for Hewlett-Packard, I took profound observations of the people who were 20-30 years older than me. If I continued on my career track, I'd be them in my 50's. What scared me was that they lived for the weekends, their workdays consisted of meaningless corporate meetings, and they acted like bureaucrats. My future looked like gray hairs and timeshares.

The grey hairs around me were the perfect pattern interrupt to force me into action. Before this realization, I was scared to fail at HP. Each year my annual review came up, I'd sit down with my manager and try to convince him why I was valuable enough to receive that small raise. Every year was the same story; the promise of a pay increase, then the usual excuse: "The company is going through a restructuring, we'll revisit your raise in 6 months."

Then came the email that lit the fire. Meg Whitman (CEO of HP at the time) got a pay increase that put her near $20 million per year, with $4.86 million of it from salary. At the time, she was the CEO, and the pay increase was because she was getting appointed as a board member. Failure didn't matter anymore, because, with all the "restructuring," and all the layoffs around me, she still got a massive raise.

I blessed Meg's success and got fired up at the idea of making that income, while not being chained like her, to the massive "cruise ship" that is HP. This experience gave me an invaluable lesson: A dull and freedomless existence is the real enemy, not a fear of failure. My senior leaders were *realistic* for years, well into their late fifties and early sixties. The most physically active years of their lives were over, and it was time for me to save my life and get *unrealistic* fast. This next part of the story can set you free.

Your Freedom Blueprint

Take these 3 points to heart as we design you a blueprint that will lay the foundation for the freedom and stimulation you desire.

- Your desires cannot be foggy and broad. You need steps to follow.
- Being *realistic* hasn't gotten you the life you desire, and it never will; you need a new path.
- Your fulfillment will come from *experiences* more than *things*. You need more time freedom to do meaningful activities that stimulate you, not just more stuff. You can have both with the process coming up.

Pen Pals With Warren Buffett?

Most ordinary people believe that hugely successful people are untouchable; It's not true. As an example, I'm going to share a story and a process you can use to raise the level of your network.

The most convenient excuse for ordinary people is that "It's all about who you know." It's an easy way for people to convince themselves that they don't know the right people, so they can't succeed. Influential people won't knock on your door and chase after you. Also, successful people didn't start at the top with a robust network of people; it wasn't some magical birthright they received.

ContactAnyCelebrity.com

The military is *one team, one fight*. Your success is the team's achievement, and the group shares your failures; nobody is different. In 2016, I had a deep desire to stand out and accomplish something that nobody else had. I wanted to feel different than everyone else. Most people forked in one of two directions: some wanted to do 20 years and retire, the rest were itching to get out at the end of their contract.

Our unit was staring down a 9-month deployment in the middle east, and I wanted to deliver a jolt of morale. Coincidentally, I was also reading "The Snowball-Warren Buffett And The Business of Life." The combination of these two events led to the extraordinary situation you're about to read.

Before Buffett, I never reached out to any public figures. When I was telling people that I was going to contact Warren and get on his radar, I got all kinds of pushback. People asked me who I think I am reaching him; they said to be realistic, that he's too busy, and I'm wasting time. Funny, everyone had an opinion, without any experience; but no one ever tried what I was attempting.

With no starting direction, I did what any ambitious millennial would do. I googled, "how to contact Warren Buffett." Here's what I learned: Wikihow has a step-by-step article to contact him, where they admit, "a reply is never guaranteed." That didn't deter me, but it wasn't enough information.

Then, I stumbled on Jordan McAuley and his company ContactAnyCelebrity.com. Game changer. The site gave me reliable information on Buffett and empowered me to craft a written letter to pique his attention.

Long story short, the letter asked Warren Buffett for more context on some personal stories in his book. It dove into details about the military, our service, and his contributions to the United States as a businessman. Then I thought, what gift can a person give that fits in an envelope, and a billionaire can't get? It turns out that's a pretty tough question.

Knowing that Warren loves to collect things, the idea came to me out of nowhere. I inserted a military coin awarded to me for winning a soldier event. It was one of my prized possessions from the military. For the following two weeks, I checked my mailbox diligently; I got to know the mailman's schedule as well as he did, but nothing came.

What did I do? Why did I give up my favorite award? Everyone was right; he's too busy! So I chalked it up as a learning experience and completely forgot that I wrote to him. Until that fateful summer day, when I opened the mailbox to a letter from 3555 Farnam St, Omaha, NE. It was from Berkshire Hathaway's headquarters. Did Buffett get my message?

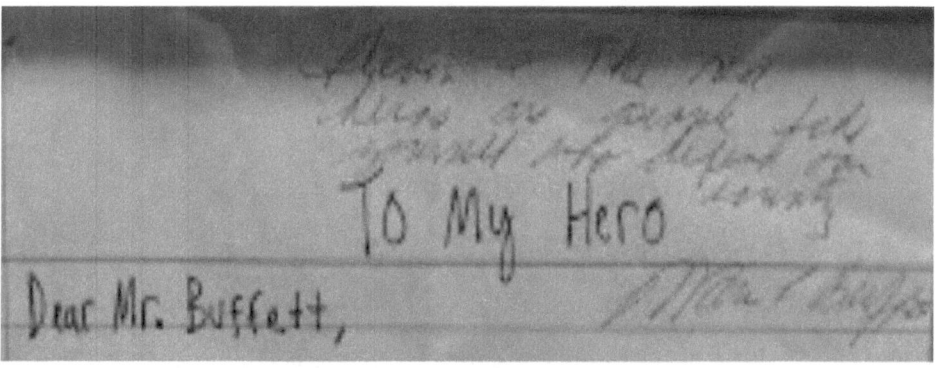

This picture is a snip of Buffett's reply, it says, "The real heroes are people like yourself who defend our country." -Warren Buffett

So much for *not* having time for others, as everyone told me. Not only did Warren make time, but he also took the time to praise and encourage us with his message. Remember how I said I wanted to stand out? A few weeks after I received the letter, our unit got called in for a morale-building exercise. I'll never forget when our leadership stood up in front of us and asked us each to tell the group something positive that happened to them this week. Imagine when my turn came, and I got to stand up in front of my friends, my brothers, and my sisters in arms to share and show them a personal letter from Warren Buffett for each of them.

My unit lost it! It was so unexpected, so positive, so refreshing that you could feel the energy explode in the room. That day, I left hundreds of soldiers better than I found them, all at once. There has never been a moment in my life where I felt more fulfilled.

And it never would have happened if I had listened to the noise that some people are untouchable and it's all about who you know. You can do remarkable things, anything you want, consider this your proof.

Doing Your Freedom Math

We live on an economic planet. No matter what you want to be, you need money to live. I'm going to teach you a freedom formula to calculate the income you need to achieve financial freedom.

Here it is: *Be + Do + Have* + (2.5x your monthly expenses). We need to add the economic costs of who you want to *become*, what you want to *do* with your extra time, and what you want to *have*; this is your fulfillment figure.

Then, we'll take your fulfillment figure and add 2.5 times your regular monthly expenses. With this formula, you'll know the exact number needed for freedom. After that, we'll get you on track to pass that figure.

Always do the math first, and create the strategy around the math second. First, set a date for your goal. How far out is your goal? Three months? 6? 12? I recommend between 6-24 months.

Next, create a list from 1-3 and write three things you want to *become* in that timeframe. For example, you may want to become a top chef, a botanist, and an animal rights activist.

Third, create another list of no more than three things you want to *do* in your timeframe. For instance, you might want to take a 7 hour VIP tour of Disneyland, surprise your whole family with dinner at Nobu, or write a book.

Fourth, create a list of no more than three things you want to *have* in your timeframe. This list will include the *stuff* you want. Examples include a virtual reality headset, a new Range Rover, or a Dyson vacuum.

Your lists can include anything you want. There are no limitations, there are no wrong answers, and there are no feelings of guilt allowed. Think of this as your guilt-free exercise. If you want to do a vacation in Italy with fine wines, don't write about going on a church mission because you feel guilty for your desires. Don't think, just write what comes to mind.

Got it? Fantastic! Now, as you know, it's no secret that most of what you write will cost money, especially what you want to *have* and what you want to *do*.

To the right of what you want to *become*, write what you want to be able to *do,* and then the cost. Finally, add up the total. We always want to *become* something, so that we can *do* something we couldn't before. Here's how this looks:

Top-chef (become) = Master 10 difficult culinary dishes including consommé devilish (do) = $3,246 at Henry Ford College (cost).

Botanist (become) = Master tissue culture (do) = $250.95 for a tissue culture micro clone kit (cost).

Animal rights activist (become) = Volunteer at your local animal shelter (do) = $0 (cost).

The total cost to become a top chef, botanist, with a heart for animal rights is $3496.95 plus your time.

Next, to the right of the cost, write the smallest step you can take to get started with each *"be, do, have"* item. Then, set a deadline to do it. For the top chef, I would write, "go to the Henry Ford College website and schedule a phone consultation within seven days from today." Then I would progress on that step, and plan out the next level, for example, "visit the Henry Ford College for a tour of the facility, within fourteen days from today." Follow a logical progression of steps.

Once you've written out your steps for each of your items, it's time to do the math. Remember that *Be* + *Do* + *Have* + (2.5x your monthly expenses). So, the fulfillment formula is $3496.95 +(2.5x your monthly expenses). If my monthly expenses are $4,000, then $3496.95 + (4,000) = $7496.95

That figure is MUCH less than the millions of dollars that people *think* they need to live a fulfilling life.

Take the final fulfillment figure and divide it by 30 days in a month.

$7496.95/30 = $249.90 per day. If these were your dreams, you would only need to earn $249.90 per day to have what you want. Now that you have the math, you can create your strategy around the math.

How can you take the work you already do and create branches of cash-flow from it? For example, a full-time nurse could create an online course in their spare time to teach proper wound care. How about a full-time cook that writes a cookbook of their favorite recipes and publishes it online as an ebook? Whatever you do, think about how you can create passive income *without* a second job, or additional time at work. Seek to have money, technology, and other people replace your time at work. When you put money, technology, and other people to work for you, you're free to expand your freedom and do what fulfills you.

Next Steps

Also by Wes Lee

Impactful Leadership

You Are Rich

You Are Successful

You Are Free

Professional Persuasion

The Brave Bunch (Children's Book)

Read more at amazon.com/author/wes_lee

About the Author

Wes Lee is a passionate advocate for success with over a decade of experience, and a business degree from Hawaii Pacific University. Best known for his leadership in the Army, and operat-ing multiple successful businesses, including lending money in 42 states, starting a business that significantly reduces health-care costs and taking ownership in a life insurance company. Lee's books take his hard-won experience and translate it into easy recipes you can follow to achieve massive breakthroughs. His site https://twitter.com/wes_lee_success shares strategies and resources to have everything you want from life while get-ting paid handsomely. Wes loves living in Kapolei, Hawaii (a personal dream) with his wife, and digging his toes in the sand at the lagoons of Ko'olina.

Follow at:

https://www.tiktok.com/@weslee1988

Bibliography

500 years of technology in the home. (1983). In D. Yarwood. London: Batsford Ltd.

A history of microwave heating applications. IEEE Transactions on Microwave Theory and Techniques. (1984). In J. Osepchuk.

Alder, J. (2019, March 6). *Randy Moss Career Controversies*. Retrieved from Liveabout.com: https://www.liveabout.com/randy-moss-antics-1335699

All That's Interesting Editors. (2014, January 6). *Seven Of The World's Most Talented Kids*. Retrieved from allthatsinteresting.com: https://allthatsinteresting.com/worlds-most-talented-kids/2

Amabile, T., Noonan Hadley, C., & Kramer, S. J. (2002, August 1). *Creativity Under the*

Gun. Retrieved from Harvard Business Review: https://hbr.org/2002/08/creativity-under-the-gun

ArtLife Editors. (2020, June 10). *INSIDE THE FACTORY: THE STUDIO WHERE ANDY WARHOL WORKED*. Retrieved from Artlife.com: https://www.artlife.com/inside-the-factory-the-studio-where-andy-warhol-worked/

Augustyn, A. (2020, April 23). *Alessandro Volta*. Retrieved from Britannica.com: https://www.britannica.com/biography/Alessandro-Volta

Bible.com. (n.d.). *Matthew 7:14 ESV*. Retrieved April 8, 2020, from Bible.com: https://www.bible.com/bible/59/MAT.7.14.ESV

Biography.com Editors. (2019, August 28). *Grandma Moses Biography*. Retrieved from The Biography.com website: https://www.biography.com/artist/grandma-moses

Biography.com Editors. (2019, September 4). *Nikola Tesla Biography*. Retrieved from The Biography.com website: https://www.biography.com/inventor/nikola-tesla

Biography.com Editors. (2020, July 6). *Abraham Lincoln Biography*. Retrieved from The Biography.com website: https://www.biography.com/us-president/abraham-lincoln

Biography.com Editors. (2020, June 16). *Alexander Fleming Biography*. Retrieved from The Biography.com website: https://www.biography.com/scientist/alexander-fleming

Biography.com Editors. (2020, May 26). *Ed Sheeran Biography*. Retrieved from The Biography.com website: https://www.biography.com/musician/ed-sheeran

Biography.com Editors. (2020, January 7). *Jay-Z Biography*. Retrieved from The Biography.com website: https://www.biography.com/musician/jay-z

Biography.com Editors. (2020, June 23). *Michael Jordan Biography*. Retrieved from The Biography.com website: https://www.biography.com/athlete/michael-jordan

Biography.com Editors. (2020, June 24). *Nelson Mandela Biography*. Retrieved from The Biography.com website: https://www.biography.com/political-figure/nelson-mandela

Biography.com Editors. (2020, July 24). *Taylor Swift Biography*. Retrieved from The Biography.com website: https://www.biography.com/musician/taylor-swift

Borkan, A. (2014, July 18). *INVENTED IN BED: MENDELEEV'S PERIODIC TABLE OF ELEMENTS*. Retrieved from blog.casper.com: https://blog.casper.com/invented-in-bed-mendeleevs-periodic-table-of-elements/

Brown, K. (2020, August 2). *Alexander Fleming*. Retrieved from Britannica.com: https://www.britannica.com/biography/Alexander-Fleming

Classic FM. (n.d.). *Johann Ambrosius Bach (1645-1695)*. Retrieved April 17, 2020, from ClassicFM.com: https://www.classicfm.com/composers

/bach/guides/friends-family-patrons/johann-ambrosius-bach/

Copeland, B. (2019, April 4). *Ultra - Allied intelligence project*. Retrieved from Britannica.com: https://www.iwm.org.uk/history/how-alan-turing-cracked-the-enigma-code

Encyclopedia of World Biography Editors. (2007, June 25). *Grandma Moses Biography*. Retrieved 2020, from Notablebiographies.com: https://www.notablebiographies.com/Mo-Ni/Moses-Grandma.html

Falk, D. (2018, April 13). *What is relativity? Einstein's mind-bending theory explained*. Retrieved from nbcnews.com: https://www.nbcnews.com/mach/science/what-relativity-einstein-s-mind-bending-theory-explained-ncna865496

Forbes Editors. (n.d.). *#46 Ray Dalio*. Retrieved May 8, 2020, from Forbes.com: https://www.forbes.com/profile/ray-dalio/#5073fe7d663a

Forty-five years of split-brain research and still going strong. (2005). In M. Gazzaniga. Nature Reviews Neuroscience.

Frankel, M. (2019, August 30). *The 100 Best Warren Buffett Quotes*. Retrieved from The Motley Fool: https://www.fool.com/investing/best-warren-buffett-quotes.aspx

Ganapati, P. (2010, October 25). *Oct 25, 1955: Time to Nuke Dinner*. Retrieved from Wired.com: https://www.wired.com/2010/10/1025home-microwave-ovens/

Glaveski, S. (2020, March 24). *COVID19: Winners, Losers and New Business Opportunities*. Retrieved from

Medium.com: https://medium.com/steveglaveski/covid19-winners-losers-and-new-business-opportunities-38a60badf579

Green, D. (2019, July 15). *Jeff Bezos has said that Amazon has had failures worth billions of dollars — here are some of the biggest ones*. Retrieved from Business Insider: https://www.businessinsider.com/amazon-products-services-failed-discontinued-2019-3

History.com Editors. (2019, June 6). *Wright Brothers*. Retrieved from HISTORY: https://www.history.com/topics/inventions/wright-brothers#section_2

History.com Editors. (2020, 13 March). *Nikola Tesla*. Retrieved from HISTORY: https://www.history.com/topics/inventions/nikola-tesla

Hosch, W. L. (2020, August 7). *Steve Wozniak*. Retrieved from Britannica.com: https://www.britannica.com/biography/Stephen-Gary-Wozniak

Howell, E. (2017, March 30). *Einstein's Theory of Special Relativity*. Retrieved from space.com: https://www.space.com/36273-theory-special-relativity.html

Ingeoexpert. (2020, January 7). *Machu Picchu: how and when was it built*. Retrieved from Ingeoexpert: https://ingeoexpert.com/en/blog/2020/01/07/machu-picchu-how-and-when-was-it-built/

IWM Editors. (n.d.). *HOW ALAN TURING CRACKED THE ENIGMA CODE*. Retrieved July 15, 2020, from iwm.org: https://www.iwm.org.uk/history/how-alan-turing-cracked-the-enigma-code

Kiyosaki, R. (Director). (2019). *Don't Chase Money, Chase Education* [Motion Picture].

Lagree, S. (2020, February 17). *Fit at 50! Jay-Z's workout and wellness secrets revealed*. Retrieved from GQ.com: https://www.gq.co.za/culture/fitness/fit-at-50-jay-zs-workout-and-wellness-secrets-revealed-42869463

Lebowitz, S. (2018, July 9). *Inside the 27-year friendship of Bill Gates and Warren Buffett, who didn't even want to meet and now have each other on speed dial*. Retrieved from BusinessInsider.com: https://www.businessinsider.com/bill-gates-warren-buffett-friendship-2018-3

Literary Devices. (n.d.). *10 Different Themes in Taylor Swift Songs*. Retrieved June 21, 2020, from Literarydevices.net:

https://literarydevices.net/10-different-themes-in-taylor-swift-songs/

Mautz, S. (2017, February 22). *Even Bill Gates Needs a Mentor. What's Your Excuse for Not Finding One?* Retrieved from ScottMautz.com: https://scottmautz.com/even-bill-gates-needs-mentor/#:~:text=Bill%20Gates%2C%20who%20revolutionized%20the,friend%20and%20mentor%2C%20Warren%20Buffett.

Mcsweeney, K. (2019, July 5). *4 of Nikola Tesla's Predictions That Came True*. Retrieved from NorthropGrumman.com: https://now.northropgrumman.com/4-of-nikola-teslas-predictions-that-came-true/

Meares, H. (2019, August 2). *Orville and Wilbur Wright: The Brothers Who Changed

Aviation. Retrieved from The Biography.com website: https://www.biography.com/news/orville-wilbur-wright-brothers-first-flight

Nelson Mandela Foundation. (n.d.). *Biography of Nelson Mandela*. Retrieved February 3, 2020, from NelsonMandela.org: https://www.nelsonmandela.org/content/page/biography

O'Malley Greenburg, Z. (2011, September 2). *Learning From Jay-Z's Successes -- And Failures*. Retrieved from Forbes.com: https://www.forbes.com/sites/zackomalleygreenburg/2011/09/02/learning-from-jay-zs-successes-and-failures/#4a71a8c67419

Otis, L. (2016, February 16). *A New Look at Visual Thinking*. Retrieved from Psychologytoday.com: https://www.psychologytoday.com/us/

blog/rethinking-thought/201602/new-look-visual-thinking

Ott, T. (2020, June 11). *Michael Jordan's Life Before He Became an NBA Star*. Retrieved from Biography.com: https://www.biography.com/news/michael-jordan-life-before-nba-early-career

Ott, T. (2020, May 28). *The Biography.com Website*. Retrieved from J.K. Rowling's Incredible Rags to Riches Story: https://www.biography.com/news/jk-rowling-harry-potter-author-rags-to-riches-billionaire

Pak, E. (2020, June 17). *Walt Disney's Rocky Road to Success*. Retrieved from The Biography.com Website: https://www.biography.com/news/walt-disney-failures

Principles Editors. (n.d.). *Principles for Success*. Retrieved June 28, 2020, from

Principles.com: https://www.principles.com/

Raga, S. (2018, August 6). *12 Surprising Facts About Andy Warhol*. Retrieved from Mentalfloss.com: https://www.mentalfloss.com/article/84016/12-things-you-might-not-know-about-andy-warhol

Robbins, T. (n.d.). *HOW TO TAP INTO THE POWER OF MULTIPLE MODELS AND GUIDES TO BECOME YOUR BEST SELF*. Retrieved March 12, 2020, from TonyRobbins.com: https://www.tonyrobbins.com/mind-meaning/the-mentors-who-coached-me/

Ryan Wang Editors. (n.d.). *Ryan Wang Biography*. Retrieved May 20, 2020, from The Ryan Wang Website: http://ryanwangpiano.com/about.html

SC Foundation Editors. (n.d.). *About Us*. Retrieved August 20, 2020, from shawncartersf.com: https://www.shawncartersf.com/about/

Schneider, L. (2020, April 21). *Dairy farmers dumping milk amid COVID-19: Pandemic's impact on the dairy industry*. Retrieved from Abcnews.com: https://abcnews.go.com/US/dairy-farmers-dumping-milk-amid-covid-19-pandemics/story?id=70268302

SMECC Editors. (2013, November 23). *Microwave Oven*. Retrieved from Smecc.org: http://www.smecc.org/microwave_oven.htm

Space.com Staff. (2013, January 2). *100 Billion Alien Planets Fill Our Milky Way Galaxy: Study*. Retrieved from Space.com:

https://www.space.com/19103-milky-way-100-billion-planets.html#:~:text=Our%20Milky%20Way%20galaxy%20is,more%2C%20a%20new%20study%20suggests.

Spanx. (2020, August 7). *About Us*. Retrieved July 7, 2020, from Spanx.com: https://www.spanx.com/about-us

Speed, M. (2016, November 17). *Who Inspires Tony Robbins?* Retrieved from Success.com.

Stefon, M. (2020, February 17). *Sara Blakely*. Retrieved from Britannica.com: https://www.britannica.com/biography/Sara-Blakely

The Biography.com Editors. (2020, July 29). *Johann Sebastian Bach Biography*. Retrieved from The Biography.com website:

https://www.biography.com/musician/johann-sebastian-bach

The Editors of Encyclopaedia Britannica. (n.d.). *10 Inventions That Changed Your World*. Retrieved January 27, 2020, from Britannica.com: https://www.britannica.com/list/10-inventions-that-changed-your-world

The Editors of Encyclopaedia Britannica. (2020, February 13). *Jay-Z - American rapper and entrepreneur*. Retrieved from Brittannica.com: https://www.britannica.com/biography/Jay-Z

Waldrop, M. (n.d.). *Einstein's Relativity Explained in 4 Simple Steps*. Retrieved May 2, 2020, from Nationalgeographic.com: https://www.nationalgeographic.com/news/2017/05/einstein-relativity-thought-experiment-train-lightning-genius/

Walsh, C. (2016, November 2). *9 Inventions Inspired by Dreams*. Retrieved from BedGuru: https://www.bedguru.co.uk/9-inventions-inspired-by-dreams

Wanczura, D. (2018, December 2). *Andy Warhol (1928-1987) - Biography - Ukiyo-e*. Retrieved from Artelino.com: https://www.artelino.com/articles/andy_warhol.asp

Whereisroadster Editors. (n.d.). *A brief history of Tesla Motors.* Retrieved May 12, 2020, from Whereisroadster.com: https://www.whereisroadster.com/tesla/

Wood, D. (2011, January 28). *Attitude Instead of Gratitude: The 20 Worst 'Tudes in Sports*. Retrieved from

Bleacherreport.com: https://bleacherreport.com/articles/587562-attitude-instead-of-gratitude-the-20-worst-tudes-in-sports

Wozniak, S. (2018, January 3). *Blue Box*. Retrieved from Woz.org: http://www.el.woz.com/letters/blue-box/

www.ingramcontent.com/pod-product-compliance
Lightning Source LLC
Chambersburg PA
CBHW020628220526
45464CB00001B/60